Christian Groups
Seder Guide

Uncovering the Eucharist's Roots
Through the Passover Meal

Dominic Sultana

Christian Groups Seder Guide: Uncovering the Eucharist's Roots Through the Passover Meal

Copyright © 2024 by Dominic Sultana. All rights reserved. No part of this book may be reproduced or transmitted in any form or by any means, including photocopying, without the prior written permission of the author, except for brief quotations in reviews.

Scripture quotations are taken from various Bible translations and are used for educational and religious purposes under the Fair Use provision. All rights to these translations are retained by their respective publishers.

The text is written by Fr Dominic and refined with the assistance of AI systems. Images within the book are created using ChatGPT.

For group use, it is recommended that each participant have their own personal copy, either in print or digital format, to fully engage with the material and facilitate a deeper shared experience. Unauthorized reproduction, including photocopies for group use, is strictly prohibited.

GodMediation PUBLICATIONS

https://www.godmediation.world

To those who seek a deeper understanding of our faith,
and to the small groups who gather in fellowship,
this work is dedicated.

May your journey through these sacred traditions
bring you closer to the heart of Christ and
the richness of the Eucharist.

Contents

Introduction 9

Part 1: The Sedar Tradition 13
The Sacred Meal 15
From Exodus to Tradition 19
The Steps of the Seder 23
Christ's Last Supper 30

Part 2: Christ's Teachings During His Last Seder 35
The New Commandment: Love One Another 37
The Promise of the Holy Spirit 42
Abiding in Christ, the True Vine 48
Christ's Prayer for His Disciples 56

Part 3: Preparing The Seder 61
The Ritual Preparations 63
Setting the Table 68
The Dynamics and Roles 73
The Spiritual Atmosphere 78

Part 4: The Seder Rite 87

Beginning the Seder 88

Opening Prayer 91

A Song of Praise 94

Blessing and First Cup 96

Washing of the Feet 98

Breaking of the Matzah 102

The Renewal of All Creation – Spring 103

The Story of the Exodus 105

The Ten Commandments 123

Washing with a Blessing 125

The Blessing and Breaking of the Bread 126

The Bitter Herbs 127

The Hillel Sandwich 128

The Festive Meal 129

Christ's Words at the Last Supper 131

Eating the Afikoman 134

The Cup of Redemption 136

Reflecting on the Institution of the Eucharist 138

Elijah's Cup 140

Blessing of the Bitter Herbs 142

A Song of Gratitude: The Dayenu 144

Recognizing the Fullness of God's Grace 146

The Cup of Freedom 152

Looking Forward: Next Year in Jerusalem 154

Closing Songs 155

Part 5: The Eucharist and The Seder 161

Understanding the Eucharist Through the Seder 162

Part 6: Group Study Guide 175

Lesson 1: Discovering the Roots 178
Lesson 2: Jesus' Final Teachings 183
Lesson 3: Preparing the Table 188
Lesson 4: From Seder to Eucharist 194

Conclusion 199

Appendix... 202

Recipes 204
   Matzot (Unleavened Bread) 205
   Beẓot (Eggs) 206
   Charoset 207
   Roast Lamb 208
Glossary of Terms 211
Church Documents 214
Annotated Bibliography 216
Clarifications 219
About the author 223

Introduction

Imagine being part of a tradition that stretches back thousands of years, passed down from generation to generation, holding within it the stories, struggles, and faith of an entire people. The Seder meal is just that—**a sacred gathering, rich in history and meaning.** For centuries, it has been central to the Jewish faith, commemorating the night when God delivered the Israelites from slavery in Egypt. Yet, for us as Christians, the Seder is also deeply connected with the Last Supper of Jesus Christ, where He instituted the Eucharist.

The primary purpose of this book is to guide Christian groups in practicing the Seder meal within the context of our faith. This is more than just a ritual; it's an opportunity to deepen our understanding of Christ's sacrifice and His fulfillment of God's promises. This resource offers a comprehensive introduction to the Seder, exploring its significance in both the Jewish tradition and in light of Christ's Last Supper. It provides a detailed explanation of Jesus' words and actions during that profound evening, alongside a step-by-step guide to the Seder rite.

At its heart, the Seder meal is **a celebration of freedom**—freedom from slavery, sin, and death. Every item on the Seder table, every prayer, and every action is a reminder of God's saving power and His unwavering love for His people. As we incorporate the words of Christ and the events of the Last Supper into this ancient tradition, we gain a richer understanding of the Eucharist, the greatest gift Christ left us.

How This Resource Can Be Used:

- **For Group Study:** Ideal for groups to explore the Seder meal in five sessions—three for preparation, one for the meal, and a final one for reflection on the Eucharist (see Part 6: Group Study Guide).

- **Perfect for Lent and Easter:** Aligns with the themes of preparation, sacrifice, and resurrection, making it especially suitable for these seasons.

- **Flexible Options:** Groups can choose to focus on the full program or just the meal itself, depending on their preference.

- **Great for Small Groups:** Smaller groups can use the Seder as an opportunity to invite family members, especially those with young children, for a shared experience of faith.

Why This Meal Matters:

- **Teaches Us About Freedom:** The Seder meal teaches us about freedom and God's promise of salvation.

- **Connects to the Last Supper:** It connects us to Jesus' Last Supper, showing us the origins of the Eucharist.

- **Deepens Our Faith:** By understanding the Seder, we can deepen our appreciation of the Eucharist today.

As you journey through this book, my hope is that you will not just learn about the Seder meal but feel its significance in your heart. This is more than history—it's a sacred practice that brings us closer to God, allowing us to experience His love more fully and understand the depth of Christ's sacrifice for each of us.

Let's take this journey together, discovering a deeper faith, a stronger connection to our spiritual roots, and a greater love for the Eucharist, the living memory of Christ's ultimate act of love.

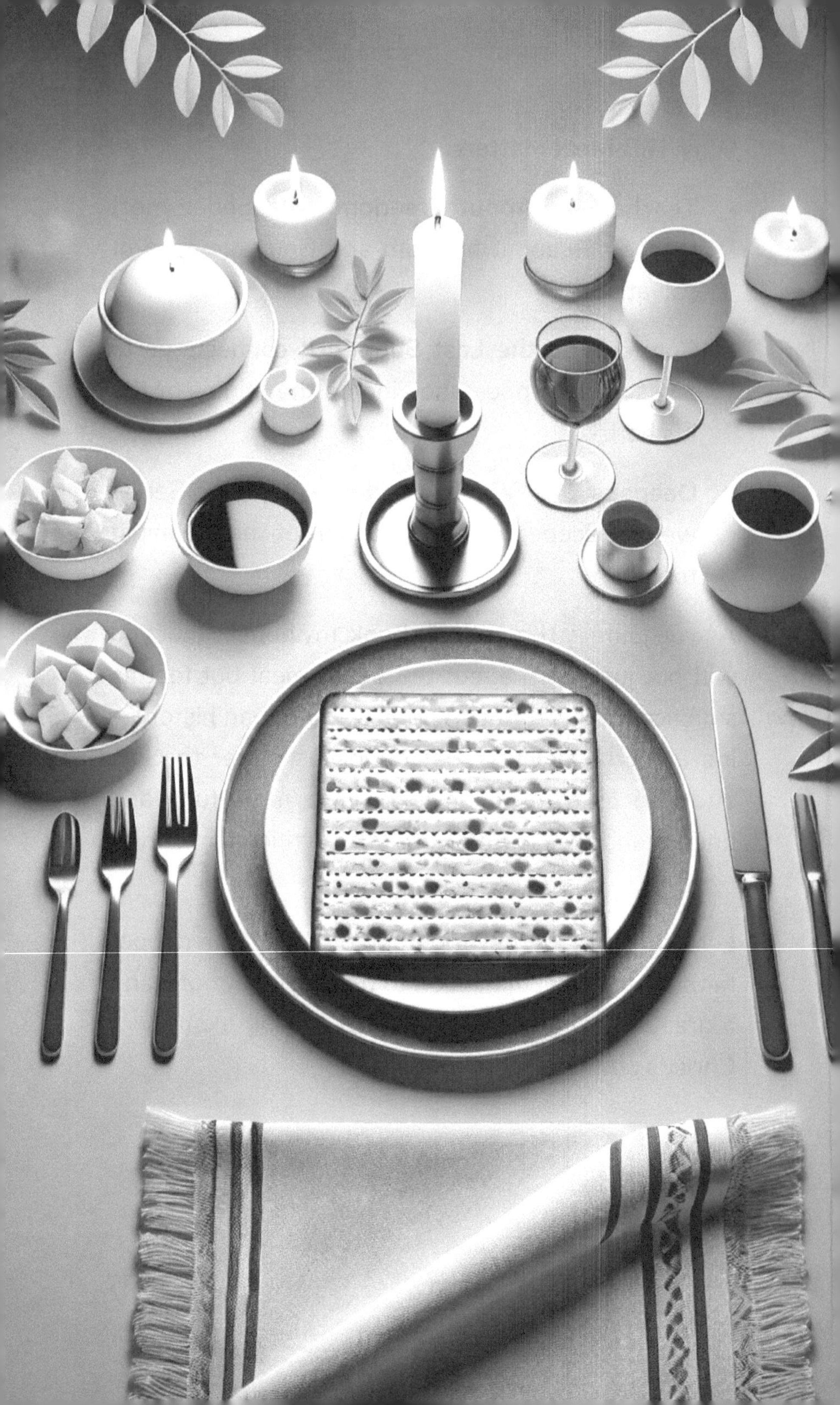

PART 1

THE SEDER TRADITION

As you get ready to celebrate the Seder, take a moment to understand the deep meaning behind this special meal. It's not just a tradition from long ago; it's a story that still speaks to us today. By learning about the Seder, you'll see how it connects to the Eucharist and the amazing love God has shown us throughout history. Let this section help your group appreciate the powerful link between the Old and New Testaments.

This section covers:

- **The Sacred Meal**: Learn where the Seder came from and why it's so important in the Jewish faith.
- **The Exodus**: Find out about Israel's escape from slavery in Egypt and how it's remembered in the Seder.
- **From the Seder to the Last Supper**: See how Jesus took this ancient tradition and gave it new meaning at the Last Supper.
- **The Seder's Lasting Impact**: Understand why the Seder is still meaningful today and how it relates to our Christian faith.

Before your group starts the Seder, take some time to read this section together. It will help make your experience more meaningful and spiritually rewarding.

The Sacred Meal

To truly understand the depth of the Eucharist, we need to take a step back in time. We need to travel to the origins of the Seder meal, a tradition that has been at the heart of the Jewish faith for centuries. This meal is more than just food on a table—it's a powerful story told through actions, prayers, and symbols. It's the story of a people who found freedom through God's miraculous intervention, and it's a story that still speaks to us today.

The Exodus: A Story of Freedom

Imagine living as a slave, where every day is marked by hardship, fear, and oppression. This was the reality for the Israelites in Egypt, a people chosen by God but trapped in bondage. But God had a plan—a plan to set them free and bring them to a land of promise.

The night before their escape, God commanded the Israelites to prepare a special meal. This meal would become known as the Passover, or Seder meal, and it was filled with deep symbolism. Each item on the table represented a part of their story:

- **The Lamb**: A symbol of sacrifice, representing the lamb whose blood was placed on their doorposts so that the angel of death would pass over their homes.

- **Unleavened Bread (Matzah)**: A reminder of the haste with which they left Egypt, with no time to let their bread rise.
- **Bitter Herbs (Maror)**: A taste of the bitterness of slavery, a reminder of the suffering they endured.

This meal wasn't just about remembering; it was about living the story. By eating these foods and telling these stories, each generation of Jews would remember God's mighty hand in their deliverance. It was a way to keep the faith alive, to pass it down from parent to child, and to keep their identity as God's chosen people strong.

From the Seder to the Last Supper

Fast forward to the time of Jesus. The Seder meal was still central to Jewish life, and Jesus, as a faithful Jew, observed it with His disciples. But on the night before His crucifixion, He did something extraordinary—He transformed the Seder meal into something new, something that would become the heart of our Christian faith: the Eucharist.

During the meal, Jesus took the bread, blessed it, broke it, and gave it to His disciples, saying, "This is my body." Then He took the cup of wine, blessed it, and gave it to them, saying, "This is my blood, the blood of the new covenant, poured out for many."

In that moment, Jesus was not just remembering the past—He was revealing the future. He was showing that He was the true Passover Lamb, the one who would sacrifice Himself to save not just one nation, but all of humanity.

The Seder's Lasting Impact

The Seder meal is more than a relic of the past; it's a living tradition that continues to shape faith. For us as Christians, it's a window into the roots of our own practice of the Eucharist. By understanding the Seder, we gain a deeper appreciation for what Jesus did at the Last Supper and what we celebrate each time we come to the altar.

Key Takeaways

- The Seder meal is a celebration of God's deliverance and faithfulness.
- Every element of the Seder tells the story of the Exodus and points forward to Jesus' sacrifice.
- By learning about the Seder, we can deepen our understanding and experience of the Eucharist.

As we journey through this book, keep in mind that **the story of the Seder is also your story**. It's a story of God's love, His desire to set you free, and His invitation to share in the meal that brings life—both then and now.

From Exodus to Tradition

Understanding the depth of the Seder meal begins with its origins. The story starts in Egypt, where the Israelites lived as slaves for centuries, enduring hardship and oppression. But God had not forgotten them. He heard their cries and decided it was time to set them free.

The night before their escape, God commanded the Israelites to prepare a special meal. They were to sacrifice a lamb without blemish and mark their doorposts with its blood. This sign would protect them from the final plague—the death of every firstborn in Egypt. Inside their homes, they ate the Passover meal—roasted lamb, unleavened bread, and bitter herbs—while preparing to leave Egypt in haste. That night, God delivered them from slavery, leading them toward the Promised Land. This event, the Exodus, became the defining moment in Israel's history, and the Passover meal was established as a lasting tradition to be observed each year.

As the years passed, the Passover meal evolved into the Seder, a structured ritual that guides participants through the story of the Exodus. "Seder" means "order," reflecting the careful sequence of prayers, readings, and symbolic foods that make up the meal. **Each element of the Seder helps participants relive the experience of the Exodus and remember God's mighty deeds.**

The Seder became **a family-centered tradition**, celebrated in homes rather than the Temple. It provided a way for parents to pass on the story of God's deliverance to their children, ensuring that each new generation would understand and cherish their heritage.

The structure of the Seder includes:

- **The Four Cups of Wine**: Representing the four promises of redemption God made to Israel.

- **The Eating of the Matzah**: Unleavened bread that recalls the haste of the Israelites' departure from Egypt.

- **The Maror (Bitter Herbs)**: A reminder of the bitterness of slavery.

- **The Recitation of the Haggadah**: The telling of the Exodus story, often with questions and answers to engage the children.

These traditions have been carefully preserved over the centuries, allowing Jewish families to connect with their ancestors and with God in a deeply personal way.

The Seder is more than a meal; it's a living tradition that has been celebrated for thousands of years. It's a powerful reminder of God's faithfulness and His desire to set His people free. For Christians, understanding the Seder is crucial because it forms the backdrop to the Last Supper, where Jesus, Himself a Jew, observed this sacred meal with His disciples.

Looking at the Seder through the eyes of faith reveals that it's not just about remembering the past; it's about experiencing the ongoing story of God's redemption. Just as the Israelites were freed from physical slavery, we are invited to experience freedom from the bondage of sin through Jesus Christ.

Key Points to Remember

- The Seder meal began with the first Passover, a night of deliverance from Egypt.
- Over time, the Seder became a carefully structured ritual that helped Jewish families remember and celebrate God's saving power.
- The Seder is the foundation of the Last Supper, where Jesus instituted the Eucharist, offering us a new kind of freedom.

With this understanding, the structure of the Seder becomes more than just a ritual—it is a profound journey that continues to shape faith and connect believers to God's ongoing story of salvation.

The Steps of the Seder

As we transition from understanding the roots of the Seder meal to experiencing its profound significance, it's important to recognize that the Seder is not just a meal—it's a sacred ritual rich with meaning. **Each step in this carefully structured tradition invites us to step into the story of God's deliverance of the Israelites from slavery in Egypt.** By participating in these rituals, we don't just recall the past; we actively engage with it, allowing it to shape our present faith journey.

Let's now walk through these steps together, exploring their deep significance and how they prepare our hearts for a closer connection with God.

1. Kadeish (Sanctification)

The Seder begins with Kadeish, a blessing over the first cup of wine. This isn't just any blessing; it's a special moment that sets the tone for the entire evening. By blessing the wine, we sanctify the meal—meaning we recognize it as holy and dedicated to God. This act reminds us that the time we are about to spend together is sacred. It's not just about the food; it's about entering into a holy experience where we thank God for His blessings and prepare our hearts for what's to come.

2. Urchatz (Washing of the Hands)

After the blessing, we move on to Urchatz, the washing of hands. This washing is done in silence and without a blessing, serving as a symbolic act of purification. It's a way to cleanse ourselves physically and spiritually before continuing with the meal. Just as we wash our hands, we're also invited to reflect on the need for inner cleanliness—clearing our minds and hearts of distractions so we can fully enter into the sacred story.

3. Karpas (Dipping of the Vegetable)

Next, we take a vegetable—often parsley—and dip it in salt water. This step is called Karpas. The vegetable represents the humble beginnings of the Israelites, and the salt water symbolizes the tears they shed during their time of slavery in Egypt. As we taste the saltiness, we are reminded of the bitterness of bondage and the sweetness of the freedom that God eventually provided. It's a small taste of the sorrow that makes the joy of deliverance even more profound.

4. Yachatz (Breaking the Matzah)

In the Yachatz step, we break the middle piece of matzah (unleavened bread) into two parts. One half is set aside to be eaten later as the afikoman (which we'll come back to), and the other half stays on the table. This act of breaking the bread is powerful—it symbolizes the brokenness of the Israelites under slavery, but it also points to the hope of redemption. By breaking the matzah, we acknowledge the pain of the past while looking forward to the wholeness that God promises.

5. Maggid (The Story)

Maggid is the storytelling part of the Seder, where we recount the story of the Exodus—the central narrative of God's deliverance. This is the heart of the Seder, where we read, pray, and ask questions to bring the story to life. It's not just about recalling facts; it's about connecting with the narrative on a personal level. Each participant, especially the youngest, plays a role in this retelling, making the story a living tradition that connects us to our ancestors and to God's saving action.

6. Rachtzah (Washing with a Blessing)

After the story, we wash our hands again—this time with a blessing. This step, known as Rachtzah, symbolizes a deeper level of purification as we prepare to eat the matzah and continue with the meal. It's a reminder that the journey of faith is ongoing, requiring us to continually cleanse our hearts and renew our commitment to God.

7. Motzi (Blessing Over the Bread)

The Motzi is the blessing over the matzah, recognizing God as the provider of all food. This traditional blessing acknowledges that everything we have comes from God's hand. As we pause to say this blessing, we express our gratitude for His sustenance, both physical and spiritual. It's a moment to remember that God is our provider and to give thanks for the grace that sustains us.

8. Matzah (Eating the Matzah)

Following the blessing, we eat the matzah. This unleavened bread is a powerful symbol of the Israelites' hurried departure from Egypt, when there wasn't time to let the bread rise. Eating the matzah is a way of participating in that story, tasting the urgency and the trust that was required to follow God's command. It's a simple yet profound act that connects us directly to the faith and obedience of those who came before us.

9. Maror (Bitter Herbs)

Maror, or bitter herbs, are eaten next to remind us of the bitterness of slavery. The sharp taste, often from horseradish, can bring tears to our eyes, just as the suffering of the Israelites brought tears to theirs. This step is a poignant reminder of the harshness of life in Egypt and serves as a moment of empathy for all who suffer. It also deepens our appreciation for the freedom and redemption that God provides.

10. Korech (The Hillel Sandwich)

In this step, we make a sandwich of matzah and maror, sometimes adding charoset—a sweet mixture representing the mortar the Israelites used in building. This sandwich, called the Korech or Hillel sandwich, brings together the bitterness of slavery and the hope of redemption, symbolized by the sweetness of the charoset. It's a tangible way to experience the contrasts of the Exodus story—the sorrow of bondage and the sweetness of deliverance.

11. Shulchan Orech (The Meal)

Now we come to the main meal, known as Shulchan Orech. This is a time of celebration, where we share a meal together in joy and thanksgiving. Traditionally, the meal includes lamb, in memory of the Passover lamb sacrificed in Egypt. As we eat, we celebrate not just the physical food before us, but also the spiritual nourishment that comes from God's deliverance. This is a moment of communal joy, where we give thanks for the freedom that God has given us.

12. Tzafun (Eating the Afikoman)

After the meal, we bring out the afikoman—the half of the matzah that was set aside earlier—and eat it. The afikoman represents the final taste of the meal, leaving us with a sense of longing for the complete redemption that is yet to come. It's a reminder that while the story of Exodus is complete, our journey with God continues, and we await the ultimate fulfillment of His promises.

13. Barech (Grace After the Meal)

Barech is the prayer of thanksgiving said over the third cup of wine. This prayer, said after the meal, is a way of wrapping up the meal with gratitude. We thank God for the food we have enjoyed and acknowledge His continuous provision in our lives. This blessing brings a spirit of closure to the meal, reminding us that all we have comes from God's gracious hand.

14. Hallel (Psalms of Praise)

After the meal, we recite or sing the Hallel—a series of psalms (113-118) filled with praise and thanksgiving to God. This step is a joyful expression of trust in God's continued protection and faithfulness. Singing these psalms is a way of joining our voices with generations of believers who have praised God for His mighty works. It's a moment of shared faith, where we look back with gratitude and forward with hope.

15. Nirtzah (Conclusion)

The Seder concludes with Nirtzah, a final prayer that the Seder has been acceptable to God. This prayer looks forward to the future, to the ultimate redemption that God has promised. The meal ends with the traditional phrase, "Next year in Jerusalem," expressing the hope that all will be gathered together in God's holy city. It's a closing that leaves us with a sense of anticipation, knowing that the story of God's deliverance is ongoing and that His promises are sure.

The Seder meal is a profound journey through the history of God's deliverance, rich with symbols that deepen our understanding of faith. Each step invites us to not only remember the past but also to engage with the present and look forward to the future fulfillment of God's promises. As we walk through the Seder, we're reminded that our faith is rooted in a story of liberation, a story that continues to unfold in our lives today. By participating in these sacred moments, we open our hearts to a deeper connection with God, allowing His grace to transform us and guide us on our spiritual journey.

Christ's Last Supper

When we think of the Last Supper, we often picture Jesus gathered with His disciples, sharing bread and wine in what would become a cornerstone of our Christian faith. But what if we saw it through the lens of the Seder meal? By understanding the connections between the Last Supper and the Seder, we can uncover a deeper meaning in the Eucharist, the sacrament that continues to nourish our faith today.

Jesus and the Seder Meal

On the night before His crucifixion, Jesus and His disciples gathered to celebrate the Passover. As observant Jews, they would have followed the customs of the Seder meal—a tradition that had been passed down through generations, all the way back to the first Passover in Egypt.

The Seder was **a time to remember God's deliverance**, but Jesus transformed it into something new. He used this meal to reveal His mission and to establish a **new covenant**—a covenant not just for Israel, but for all of humanity.

The Bread and the Wine

During the Seder, there is a moment when the bread (matzah) is broken and shared. Jesus took this familiar act and gave it new significance. He broke the bread and said, "This is my body, which is given for you. Do this in remembrance of me" (Luke 22:19). In that moment, Jesus was declaring that **He was the true Passover Lamb, the one who would be sacrificed to bring freedom—not from physical slavery, but from the bondage of sin**.

Later in the meal, Jesus took the cup of wine—likely the third cup, known as the Cup of Redemption—and said, "This cup is the new covenant in my blood, which is poured out for you" (Luke 22:20). With these words, Jesus was establishing a new covenant between God and His people, sealed not with the blood of lambs, but with His own blood.

A New Covenant

The concept of a covenant was deeply rooted in Jewish tradition. Covenants were sacred agreements between God and His people, often sealed with a ritual or sacrifice. The first Passover was part of the covenant God made with Israel, promising to be their God and to deliver them from oppression.

By invoking the language of the covenant at the Last Supper, Jesus was telling His disciples—and us—that His death would inaugurate a new covenant. This new covenant would not be limited to Israel, but would extend to all people, offering forgiveness, redemption, and eternal life.

The Ultimate Sacrifice

As the meal progressed, the significance of what Jesus was doing became clearer. He was not just leading His disciples in a traditional Seder; He was preparing them for what was to come. Jesus knew that within hours, He would be arrested, tried, and crucified. Yet, He approached this sacrifice willingly, knowing that His death would bring life to all who believe in Him.

The bread and wine of the Last Supper are not just symbols—they are a participation in the sacrifice of Jesus. Each time we celebrate the Eucharist, we are brought back to that moment in the Upper Room, where Jesus gave Himself for us.

Connecting the Seder and the Eucharist

The Last Supper was **a bridge between the old and the new**—a fulfillment of the Seder and a foundation for the Eucharist. By understanding the Seder, we can see how Jesus fulfilled the promises of God and how the Eucharist continues to bring those promises into our lives.

The Eucharist is our ongoing connection to the sacrifice of Jesus. Just as the Seder reminded the Israelites of God's deliverance, the Eucharist reminds us of our own deliverance through Christ. It is a meal of remembrance, of thanksgiving, and of hope.

Key Connections to Remember

- The Last Supper was a Seder meal, where Jesus transformed traditional symbols into powerful signs of the new covenant.

- The bread and wine of the Eucharist connect us to Jesus' sacrifice, just as the Seder connected the Israelites to the Passover.

- By celebrating the Eucharist, we participate in the new covenant and are reminded of God's promise of eternal life.

As we continue our journey, let's carry this understanding with us. The Eucharist is more than a ritual; it's a living memory of the love and sacrifice of Jesus, who gave Himself so that we might live.

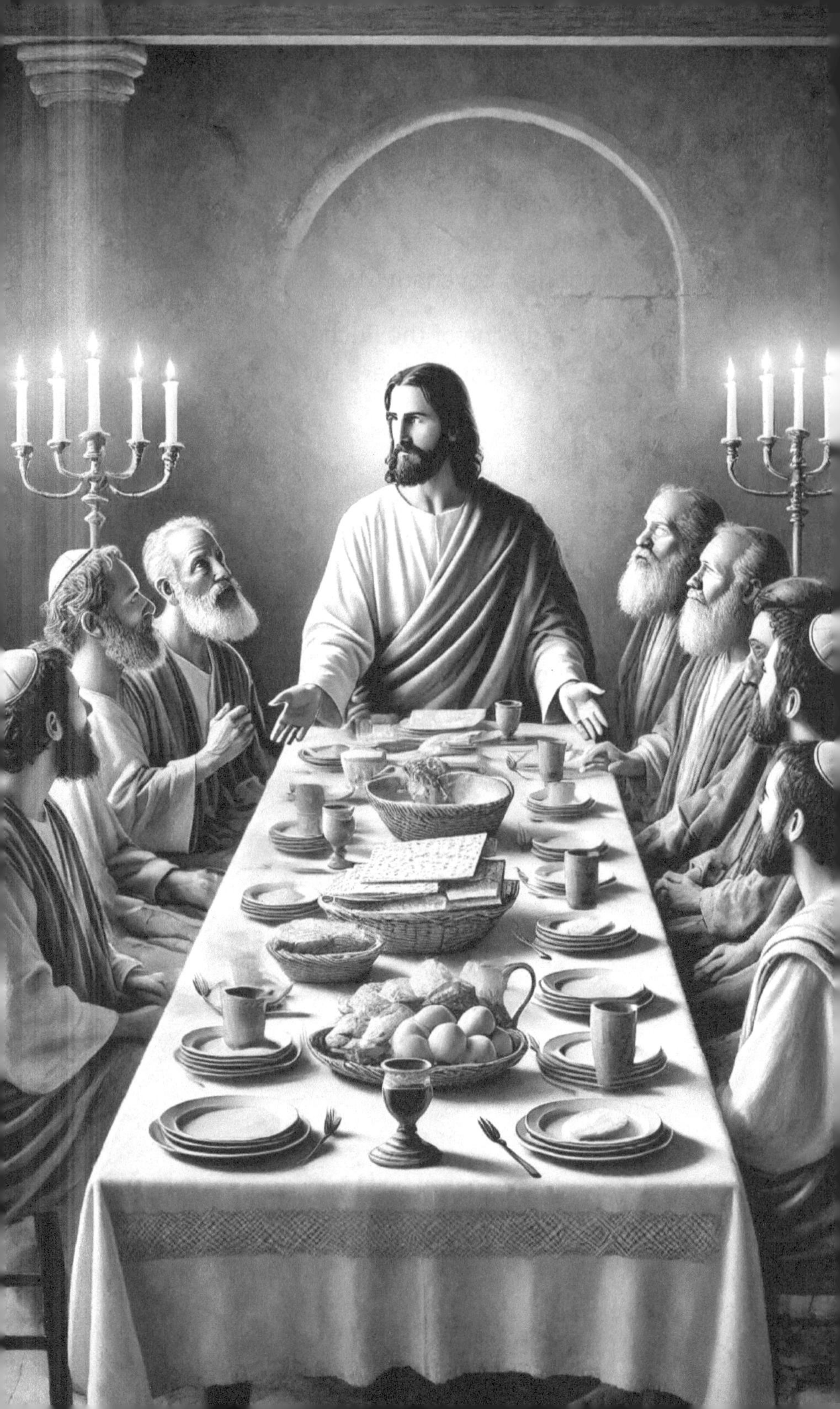

PART 2

CHRIST'S TEACHINGS DURING HIS LAST SEDER

As you prepare to reflect on the Seder, take a moment to focus on the powerful teachings that Jesus shared during His Last Supper. This wasn't just a meal; it was the final opportunity for Jesus to impart deep spiritual truths to His disciples, truths that still guide us today. By understanding these teachings, you'll gain insight into the profound connection between the Last Supper and the Seder, and how Jesus' words continue to shape our faith.

This section covers:

- **The New Commandment: Love One Another**: Discover how Jesus redefined love during the Last Supper, making it the foundation of Christian life.
- **The Promise of the Holy Spirit**: Learn about the comfort and guidance Jesus promised through the Holy Spirit, ensuring His presence with us always.
- **Abiding in Christ, the True Vine**: Explore the vital connection between Christ and His followers, and how staying connected to Him helps us bear fruit.
- **Christ's Prayer for His Disciples**: Reflect on Jesus' heartfelt prayer for unity, protection, and sanctification for His disciples and all believers.

Before your group begins the Seder, take time to read and meditate on these teachings together. Doing so will deepen your understanding and make your experience of the Seder more meaningful and enriching.

The New Commandment: Love One Another

As we reflect on what Jesus said at the Last Supper, we encounter one of the most profound teachings Jesus shared with His disciples—a commandment that has become the foundation of Christian life:

> *"I give you a new commandment, that you love one another. Just as I have loved you, you also should love one another. By this, everyone will know that you are my disciples if you have love for one another"* (John 13:34-35).

These words, spoken in the quiet of the Upper Room, were not just instructions for the moment but a timeless directive that continues to shape the heart of Christian community.

The Foundation of Christian Life and Community

During the Seder meal, Jesus chose this moment to deepen the understanding of love within the context of His new covenant. The Passover was traditionally a time of remembrance—a time to recall God's deliverance of Israel from slavery in Egypt and His covenant with His people. However, Jesus changed this occasion by introducing a new dimension of that covenant, one that would be centered on love—not just any love, but a love that mirrors His own.

This commandment to love one another was not simply an additional rule to follow. It was—and still is—**the very essence of what it means to live as a disciple of Christ**. The love Jesus speaks of here is not a casual affection or a love based on feelings alone. It is a deliberate, self-giving love that seeks the good of the other, even at great personal cost. This kind of love is sacrificial, mirroring the love that Jesus Himself demonstrated throughout His life and ministry, and which He would soon embody most fully in His sacrifice on the cross.

The Sacrificial Nature of Christ's Love

When Jesus said, "Just as I have loved you," He was pointing to a love that is profoundly sacrificial. In the hours following the Last Supper, Jesus would go on to lay down His life for His disciples and for all humanity—**a love that knows no bounds** and is willing to endure suffering and death for the sake of others. This is the standard of love that Jesus set for His followers.

This moment at the Last Supper was not just another teaching moment; it was a *congedo*—a farewell, a final gathering where Jesus wanted to leave His testament with His disciples. Knowing that His time with them was short, **He wanted to ensure that they understood the heart of His message and mission:**

love. This commandment to love one another as He had loved them was His final testament, the legacy He wanted to leave with them as they faced the challenges ahead.

In washing the feet of His disciples earlier that evening, Jesus had already shown them that **true love involves humility and service.** He, their Master and Teacher, took on the role of a servant, performing a task that was considered lowly and menial. This act was a living parable of the kind of love He was commanding them to have for one another—a love that serves, a love that does not seek its own glory, but rather seeks to uplift and support others.

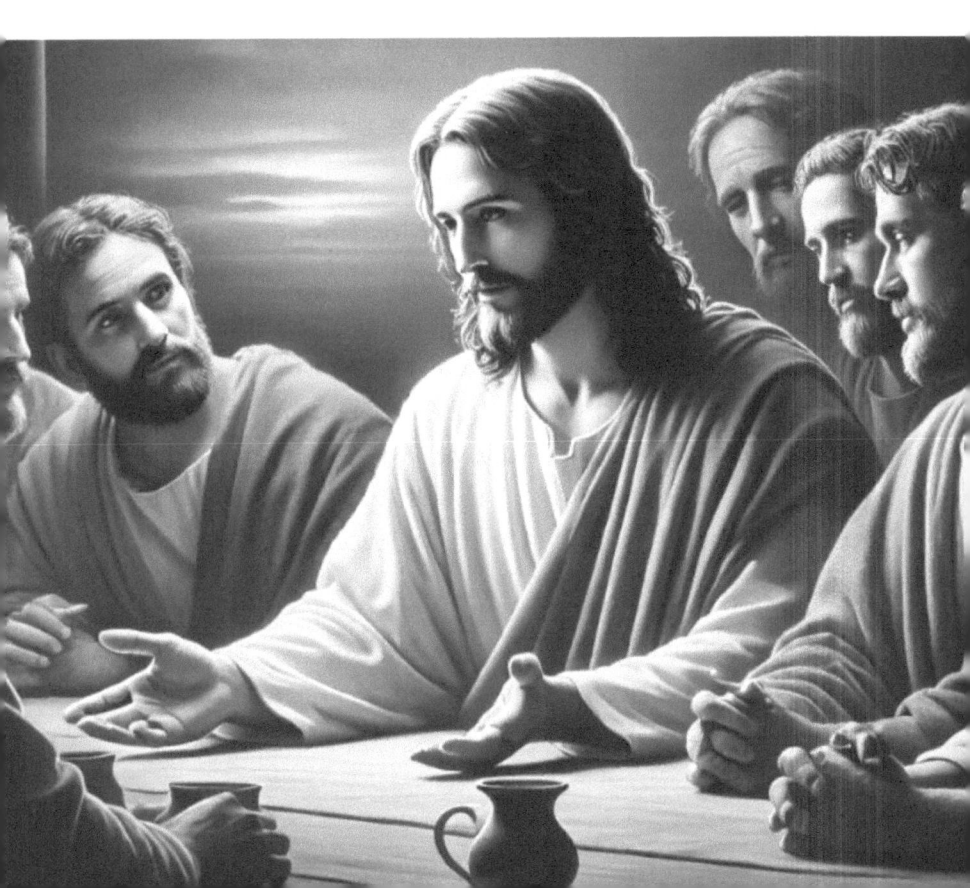

This sacrificial love is the hallmark of Christian discipleship. It is a love that goes beyond mere words and is expressed in actions—actions that reflect the selflessness and generosity of Christ Himself. It is a love that is willing to forgive, to bear with others in their weaknesses, and to put the needs of others before one's own.

Living Out the New Commandment

Living out this commandment to love one another as Christ has loved us is **no small task**. It requires a continual dying to self, a willingness to let go of pride, and an openness to being vulnerable and compassionate. In a world that often promotes self-interest and competition, this commandment stands as a radical call to a different way of living—a way that is marked by selfless love and deep, abiding community.

This love is not something we can generate on our own. It is **a love that is born out of our relationship with Christ, nurtured by the Holy Spirit, and sustained by our ongoing connection to the source of all love—God Himself.** As we draw closer to Christ, we are enabled to love others as He has loved us. This love becomes the identifying mark of our discipleship, the evidence to the world that we truly belong to Him.

In the context of the Seder meal, as we prepare to reflect on the profound events that unfold in the life of Christ, let us take to heart this new commandment. Let it be the lens through which we view our relationships, our actions, and our own journey of faith. As we strive to love one another as Christ has loved us, we participate in the life of God Himself, who is love.

As we move forward in this journey, may we continually return to these words of Jesus, allowing them to shape our hearts and our lives. For in loving one another, we fulfill the law of Christ and bear witness to the world of the transforming power of His love. This love is the bedrock of our Christian community, a love that goes beyond human limits and reflects the divine love that we have received through Christ.

Let this new commandment resonate in our hearts as we live out our faith, drawing others to the light of Christ through our acts of love and kindness. And as we remember the Last Supper, let us hold fast to the testament that Jesus left us, embracing the call to love one another as He has loved us.

The Promise of the Holy Spirit

As the Last Supper continued, Jesus knew that His disciples were troubled by the thought of His impending departure. **Sensing their fear and uncertainty, He offered them words of comfort and hope by promising the gift of the Holy Spirit.** In John 14:16-17, Jesus assures His disciples that although He would no longer be with them physically, they would not be left alone. Instead, they would receive the Holy Spirit, who would dwell within them, guiding, teaching, and empowering them for the journey ahead. This promise was not just for the disciples gathered around Him that night but for all believers throughout the ages.

The Advocate, the Spirit of Truth

Jesus refers to the Holy Spirit as the Advocate, a term that conveys the idea of someone who comes alongside to help, support, and defend.

> *"And I will ask the Father, and he will give you another Advocate, to be with you forever. This is the Spirit of truth, whom the world cannot receive, because it neither sees him nor knows him. You know him because he abides with you, and he will be in you"* (John 14:16-17).

This promise was a **profound reassurance** to the disciples, who were facing the uncertainty of life without Jesus' physical presence. The Holy Spirit, the Spirit of Truth, would continue the work that Jesus had begun, guiding them into all truth and reminding them of everything He had taught (John 14:26; 16:13).

The Holy Spirit's role as the Advocate is central to the Christian life. The Spirit is not just a distant force but **a personal presence who dwells within each believer**, offering guidance, comfort, and strength. This indwelling presence of the Holy Spirit is what enables us to live out our faith, to understand the Scriptures, and to follow Jesus' teachings. It is through the Holy Spirit that we experience the ongoing presence of Christ in our lives, even though He is no longer physically with us.

The Spirit's work of transformation

One of the most significant aspects of the Holy Spirit's work is the transformation that takes place in the lives of believers. **The Spirit works within us to shape our hearts and minds, conforming us to the image of Christ.** This process of transformation is what the Apostle Paul refers to as the "fruit of the Spirit" in Galatians 5:22-23—qualities such as love, joy, peace, patience, kindness, goodness, faithfulness, gentleness, and self-control. These are the characteristics that reflect the life of Christ in us, and they are evidence of the Spirit's work in our lives.

The Holy Spirit also **empowers us for service**. Just as the Spirit equipped the early disciples to carry out the mission of the Church, so too does the Spirit equip us today. Whether through spiritual gifts, acts of service, or the ability to speak words of wisdom and encouragement, the Holy Spirit enables us to fulfill our calling as followers of Christ. This empowerment is not just for a select few but is available to all who believe, enabling us to participate in God's work in the world.

A guide in times of uncertainty

The promise of the Holy Spirit is especially **comforting in times of uncertainty and difficulty**. Just as the disciples were facing an unknown future without Jesus, we too face challenges and uncertainties in our own lives. In these moments, the Holy Spirit is our guide, offering wisdom and discernment to navigate the complexities of life. The Spirit helps us to understand God's will, to make decisions that align with His purposes, and to remain faithful even when the path ahead is unclear.

Jesus' promise of the Holy Spirit also reminds us that **we are never truly alone**. The Spirit is always with us, offering comfort and peace in the midst of our struggles. This presence is a source of strength, enabling us to persevere through trials and to find hope in the midst of suffering.

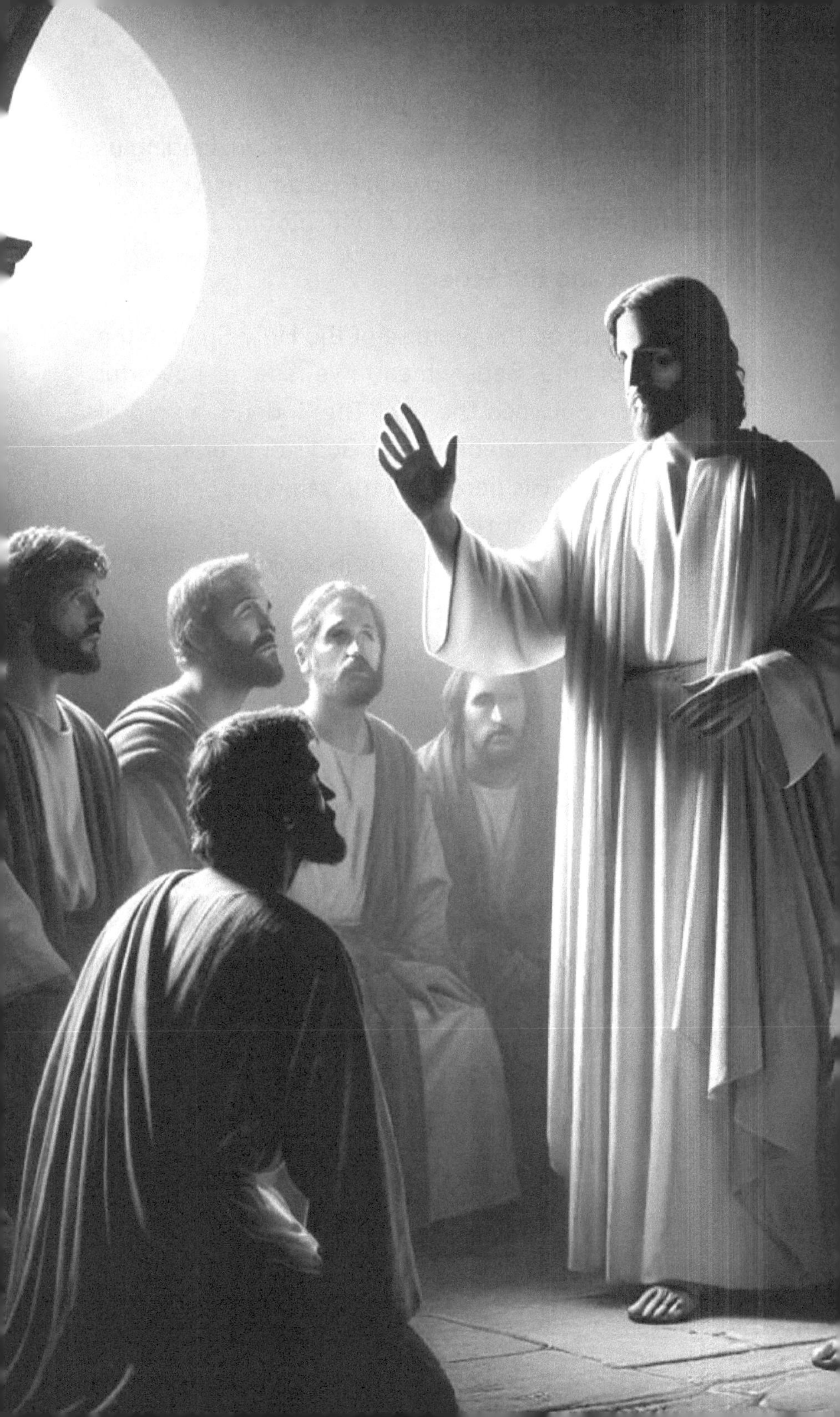

The Holy Spirit is our constant companion, leading us into a deeper relationship with God and helping us to trust in His goodness, even in difficult times.

The Spirit and the Seder

As we reflect on the promise of the Holy Spirit in the context of the Seder meal, we see a powerful connection between the two. The Seder is a time of remembrance, a celebration of God's deliverance and faithfulness to His people. In the same way, the Holy Spirit is a constant reminder of God's presence with us, guiding us and sustaining us in our journey of faith. Just as the Israelites were led by the Spirit of God through the wilderness, we too are led by the Holy Spirit in our own lives, guided by His wisdom and empowered by His presence.

As we prepare to enter into the Seder meal, let us take a moment to reflect on the gift of the Holy Spirit. Let us remember that we are not alone in our journey, but that we have been given the Spirit of Truth to guide us, to teach us, and to empower us for the work that God has called us to do. The promise of the Holy Spirit is a source of hope and strength, reminding us that we are connected to Christ and that we have been given everything we need to live a life that is pleasing to God.

The ongoing presence of Christ

The promise of the Holy Spirit is ultimately **a promise of the ongoing presence of Christ in our lives.** Through the Holy Spirit, we continue to experience the love, grace, and power of Jesus, even though He is no longer physically present with us. This presence is what sustains us in our faith, enabling us to live out the teachings of Jesus and to bear witness to His love in the world.

As we reflect on this promise, **let us be encouraged by the knowledge that we have been given the gift of the Holy Spirit, the Advocate, who is with us forever**. Let us seek to live in the fullness of this promise, allowing the Spirit to guide us, to transform us, and to empower us for the work of the Kingdom. And as we come to the Seder meal, let us do so with hearts full of gratitude for the gift of the Holy Spirit, who is the source of our life, our strength, and our hope in Christ.

Abiding in Christ, the True Vine

During the Last Supper, Jesus shared one of the most profound teachings about the relationship between Himself and His disciples: the image of the vine and the branches. He declared:

> *"I am the true vine, and my Father is the vinegrower. He removes every branch in me that bears no fruit. Every branch that bears fruit he prunes to make it bear more fruit. You have already been cleansed by the word that I have spoken to you. Abide in me as I abide in you. Just as the branch cannot bear fruit by itself unless it abides in the vine, neither can you unless you abide in me. I am the vine, you are the branches. Those who abide in me and I in them bear much fruit, because apart from me you can do nothing. Whoever does not abide in me is thrown away like a branch and withers; such branches are gathered, thrown into the fire, and burned. If you abide in me, and my words abide in you, ask for whatever you wish, and it will be done for you. My Father is glorified by this, that you bear much fruit and become my disciples"* (John 15:1-8).

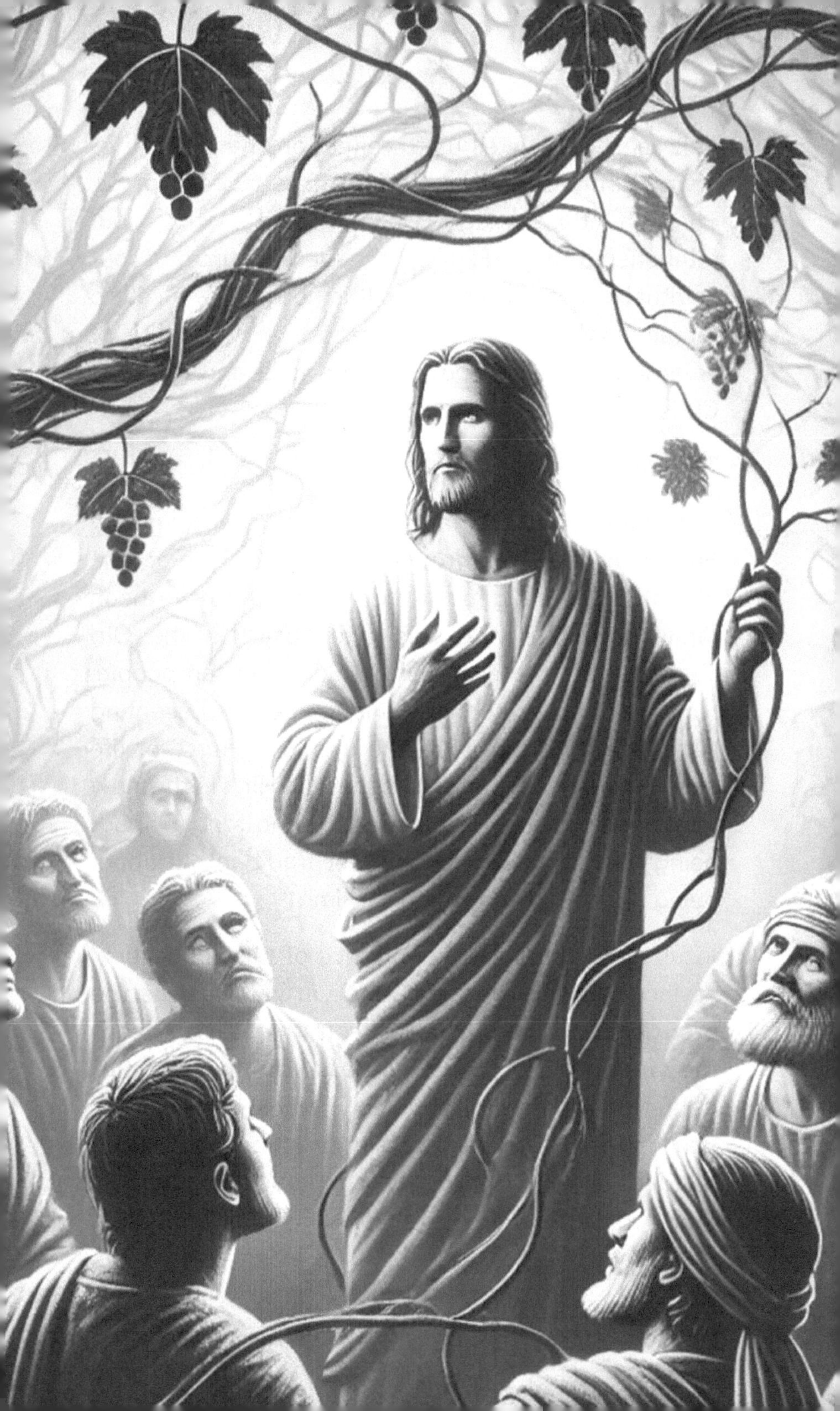

This teaching invites us to reflect on **the deep, life-giving connection that Christ offers to each of us**. Through this image, Jesus reveals that our relationship with Him is the very source of our spiritual vitality and growth. It is not merely a call to remain faithful; it is an invitation to live a life of abundance, deeply rooted in the love and grace of Christ.

The Vine and the Branches

Jesus begins by declaring, *"I am the true vine, and my Father is the vinegrower"* (John 15:1). For the disciples, the imagery of the vine would have been familiar, as the vine was often used in the Old Testament to represent Israel, God's chosen people. However, Jesus redefines this image by presenting Himself as the true vine, the ultimate source of life and sustenance for all who believe in Him. In this new relationship, belonging to Christ is no longer about being part of a specific nation or tradition but about being intimately connected to Him.

Jesus emphasizes the importance of this connection, saying, **"Abide in me as I abide in you. Just as the branch cannot bear fruit by itself unless it abides in the vine, neither can you unless you abide in me"** (John 15:4). The word "abide" means to remain or stay, highlighting the necessity of an ongoing, living relationship with Christ. Just as a branch must remain attached to the vine to receive nourishment, we must stay connected to Jesus to live lives that reflect His love and bear the fruit of the Spirit.

Bearing Fruit That Lasts

Central to Jesus' teaching is the idea of bearing fruit. He makes it clear that the purpose of our connection to Him is not just for our own benefit but so that we might bear fruit that glorifies God. ***"Those who abide in me and I in them bear much fruit, because apart from me you can do nothing"*** (John 15:5). The fruit Jesus speaks of represents the visible evidence of a life lived in union with Him—qualities like love, joy, peace, and kindness, as well as the impact we have on others through our words and actions.

Bearing fruit is not something we can achieve by our own efforts; it is the natural outcome of a life connected to Christ. Just as a branch does not produce fruit by its own effort but by drawing life from the vine, we bear fruit by staying connected to Jesus and allowing His life to flow through us. This fruit is not just for our own benefit but is meant to bless others and bring glory to God. It's a reminder that our spiritual growth is not an end in itself but a means through which God's love and grace can be shared with the world. As Jesus says, ***"My Father is glorified by this, that you bear much fruit and become my disciples"*** (John 15:8). By bearing fruit, we fulfill our calling as disciples and contribute to the unfolding of God's kingdom on earth.

The Process of Pruning

An essential aspect of this teaching is the process of pruning. Jesus explains that the Father, as the vine grower, removes every branch that bears no fruit and prunes every branch that does bear fruit to make it bear even more (John 15:2). Pruning is a gardening practice where dead or overgrown branches are cut away to promote the health and productivity of the plant. In our spiritual lives, pruning can take the form of challenges, trials, or the call to let go of certain habits, attitudes, or attachments that hinder our relationship with Christ.

Pruning is often painful because it involves loss and change. It may mean the end of certain relationships, the stripping away of comforts, or the refining of our character through difficult circumstances. However, this process is always done out of love and with the purpose of making us more fruitful. Just as a vine is pruned to ensure that it produces the best grapes, we are pruned by the Father so that we may grow in holiness and bear fruit that endures.

The purpose of pruning is not to harm us but to help us grow in ways that are pleasing to God. It is through pruning that we become stronger in our faith, more dependent on God's grace, and more fruitful in our service to others. When we face trials and difficulties, we can trust that the Father is at work, removing what is not beneficial and refining us so that we may reflect Christ more fully. As we submit to His pruning, we do so with the confidence that He knows what is best for us and that His work in our lives will lead to greater growth and greater glory for His name.

Abiding in Christ's Love

As Jesus continues, He underscores that abiding in Him is not just about bearing fruit but about living in His love. *"As the Father has loved me, so I have loved you; abide in my love"* (John 15:9). This love is the foundation of our relationship with Christ and the source of our ability to love others. Abiding in His love means remaining rooted in the knowledge and experience of His love for us, allowing that love to shape every aspect of our lives.

Jesus calls us to follow His example of self-giving love, saying, *"This is my commandment, that you love one another as I have loved you"* (John 15:12). When we abide in Christ, His love flows through us, empowering us to love others with the same sacrificial and unconditional love that He has shown us. This love is the most important fruit we can bear, and it is the true mark of discipleship.

Abiding in Christ's love also involves obedience to His commandments. Jesus says, *"If you keep my commandments, you will abide in my love, just as I have kept my Father's commandments and abide in his love"* (John 15:10). This obedience is not a burdensome duty but a joyful response to the love that Christ has shown us. It is through obedience that we remain in His love and experience the fullness of the life He offers.

Living a Life of Abundance

The image of the vine and the branches is not just a metaphor; it is a call to live a life of abundance in Christ. Jesus promises that those who abide in Him will experience the fullness of joy that comes from being in a deep, loving relationship with God. ***"I have said these things to you so that my joy may be in you, and that your joy may be complete"*** (John 15:11). This joy is not dependent on circumstances but on our connection to the source of all life and love—Jesus Himself.

As we reflect on this teaching, we are reminded of the importance of staying connected to Christ in every area of our lives. Whether in times of abundance or in times of trial, our strength, hope, and ability to bear fruit come from our relationship with Him. The Seder meal, with its focus on remembering God's deliverance and faithfulness, serves as a powerful reminder of the life-giving connection we have with Jesus, the true vine.

Conclusion

The teaching of the vine and the branches is a profound reminder of the central role that our relationship with Jesus plays in our lives. As we abide in Him, we draw life, strength, and nourishment from His presence, and we are empowered to bear fruit that glorifies God. This abiding relationship is the heart of the Christian life—a life lived in union with Christ, shaped by His love, and marked by the fruit of the Spirit.

As we prepare to enter into the Seder meal, let us commit to staying connected to Jesus, allowing His life to flow through us, and bearing fruit that blesses others and glorifies God. May we embrace the Father's pruning with trust, knowing that it is part of His loving care for us, and may we approach the Seder with hearts full of gratitude for the gift of this abiding relationship with Jesus, who is the true vine and the source of our life in God.

Christ's Prayer for His Disciples

As the Last Supper drew to a close, Jesus turned His heart and His words toward the Father in a prayer that is often referred to as the High Priestly Prayer. This profound and intimate prayer, recorded in John 17, encapsulates Jesus' deepest desires for His disciples and for all who would believe in Him through their message. It is a prayer that reveals not only His love for His followers but also His commitment to the mission the Father had entrusted to Him.

The Prayer of Unity

One of the central themes of Jesus' prayer is unity. He prays, *"Holy Father, protect them in your name that you have given me, so that they may be one, as we are one"* (John 17:11). Jesus knew that His disciples would face many challenges and trials after His departure, and His prayer was that they would remain united, just as He and the Father are united.

This call to unity extends beyond the immediate group of disciples to include all who would come to believe in Christ through their witness. Jesus prays, *"I ask not only on behalf of these but also on behalf of those who will believe in me through their word, that they may all be one. As you, Father, are in me and I am in you, may they also be in us, so that the world may believe that you have sent me"* (John 17:20-21). The unity of believers is a powerful testimony to the world of the truth of the Gospel and the love of God.

The Prayer for Protection

Jesus also prays for the protection of His disciples, asking the Father to keep them safe from the evil one: *"I am not asking you to take them out of the world, but I ask you to protect them from the evil one"* (John 17:15). This protection is not about physical safety but about safeguarding their faith and their mission. Jesus knew that the world would be hostile to His message and to His followers, but He prayed that the Father would give them the strength to persevere.

This prayer for protection is also a reminder to us that while we are called to live in the world, we are not of the world. Our true home is with the Father, and our mission is to bear witness to His love and truth in a world that often rejects Him. Just as Jesus prayed for His disciples, He prays for us, asking the Father to protect us and to keep us faithful to our calling.

The Prayer for Sanctification

Another key aspect of Jesus' prayer is sanctification. He prays, *"Sanctify them in the truth; your word is truth. As you have sent me into the world, so I have sent them into the world. And for their sakes, I sanctify myself, so that they also may be sanctified in truth"* (John 17:17-19). Sanctification is the process of being made holy, set apart for God's purposes. Jesus prays that His disciples would be sanctified by the truth of God's word, and that through this sanctification, they would be equipped to carry out their mission in the world.

This prayer highlights the importance of living according to God's word and being transformed by His truth. As followers of Christ, we are called to be holy, to live lives that reflect the character of God, and to be witnesses to His truth in the world. Jesus' prayer for our sanctification reminds us that this is not something we can achieve on our own; it is a work of God in our lives, accomplished through His word and by the power of the Holy Spirit.

The Prayer for Eternal Life

Finally, Jesus' prayer expresses His desire that His disciples would be with Him where He is and that they would see His glory: **"Father, I desire that those also, whom you have given me, may be with me where I am, to see my glory, which you have given me because you loved me before the foundation of the world"** (John 17:24). This prayer is a promise of eternal life, a life that is not only about living forever but about being in the presence of God and sharing in His glory.

This promise of eternal life is at the heart of the Christian hope. It is the assurance that no matter what we face in this life, we have a future with God that is full of joy, peace, and glory. Jesus' prayer for us is that we would hold on to this hope, that we would live our lives with eternity in view, and that we would remain faithful to the end.

The Legacy of Christ's Prayer

The High Priestly Prayer of Jesus is a powerful reminder of His love for His disciples and for all who would come to believe in Him. It is a prayer that continues to resonate with us today, calling us to unity, protection, sanctification, and the hope of eternal life. As we reflect on this prayer in the context of the Seder meal, we are reminded of the deep connection between the Last Supper and the Eucharist, and of the ways in which Jesus' prayer continues to shape our lives as His followers.

As we prepare to participate in the Seder meal, let us take these words of Jesus to heart. Let us strive for unity in our communities, trust in God's protection, seek holiness through His word, and hold fast to the promise of eternal life. May the prayer of Christ for His disciples become our prayer as well, guiding us as we journey together in faith, hope, and love.

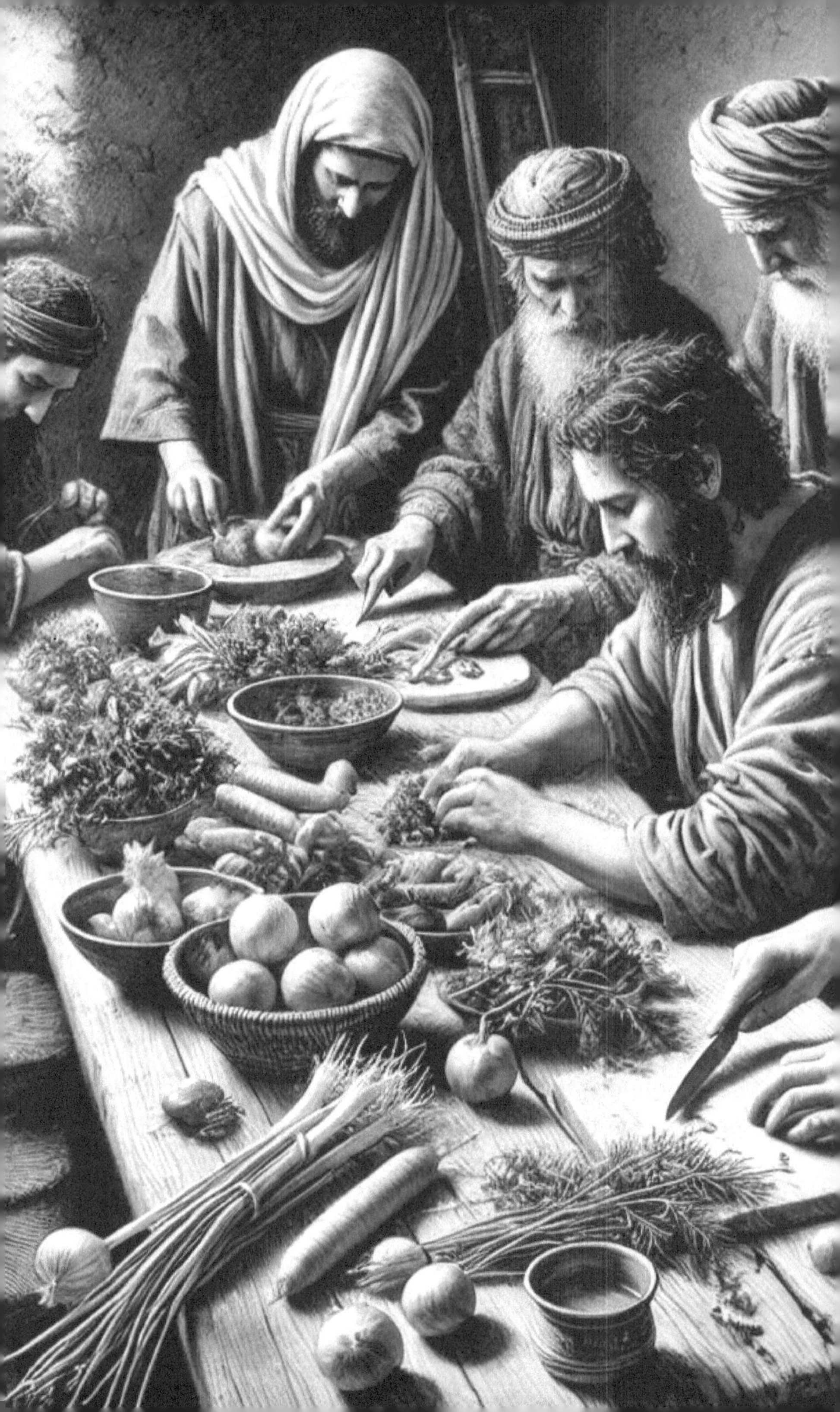

PART 3

PREPARING THE SEDER

As you prepare for the Seder, remember that this is more than just a meal—it's a profound spiritual experience that connects us with the deep roots of our faith. Every part of the preparation, from setting the table to preparing symbolic foods, invites us to enter the story of God's deliverance, bringing the ancient traditions of Passover to life today.

This section covers:

- **The Ritual Preparations**: Learn how to prepare the symbolic foods and items used during the meal, each with deep spiritual meaning.

- **Setting the Table**: Create a sacred, inviting space that reflects the significance of the occasion, enhancing the spiritual experience.

- **The Dynamics and Roles During the Seder Meal**: Understand the key roles participants play, fostering unity and engagement.

- **Creating the Spiritual Atmosphere**: Cultivate an environment that helps everyone connect deeply with the Seder's spiritual significance.

These preparations will help make your Seder a meaningful and spiritually enriching experience, where everyone participates in the ongoing story of God's faithful love and redemption.

The Ritual Preparations

The Seder meal is more than just a ritual; it is a deeply spiritual experience that invites us to engage with the foundational stories of our faith. Before the table is set, the first step is to prepare the ritual items that will be used during the meal. Each of these elements holds profound spiritual significance, transforming the Seder from a simple meal into a sacred act of worship and remembrance. The care and intention with which these items are prepared reflect our readiness to engage fully in this ancient tradition.

Matzah Preparation

The matzah, often referred to as the "bread of affliction," is central to the Seder. Traditionally, three pieces of matzah are placed together on the table, each representing different aspects of the Exodus story and the unity of the people of Israel. The middle matzah is broken during the Seder, inviting reflection on the brokenness and the hope for wholeness that comes through faith.

Handle the matzah with care, considering its fragility and simplicity. These qualities mirror the vulnerability and reliance on God that the Israelites experienced in the wilderness. The matzah reminds us that in our own lives, it is often in our moments of greatest need that we find the deepest connection to God.

Karpas and Salt Water

The preparation of the karpas, usually fresh parsley or rucola, along with the salt water, serves as an early moment of reflection in the Seder. The karpas symbolizes the freshness of spring and new beginnings, while the salt water represents the tears of the Israelites during their enslavement in Egypt.

Before the Seder begins, wash the karpas and place it in a small dish on the table, with the bowl of salt water nearby. The act of dipping the karpas into the salt water early in the Seder is not just a ritual; it is a sensory experience that connects us to the bitterness of slavery and the hope of renewal.

Maror and Charoset

The maror, typically horseradish, is prepared in small portions for each participant. Its bitter taste serves as a stark reminder of the harshness of slavery and the suffering endured by the Israelites. This bitterness is contrasted with the charoset, a sweet mixture made from apples, nuts, wine, and spices, symbolizing the mortar used by the Israelites in their forced labor.

The sweetness of the charoset reflects the hope of redemption that sustained the Israelites through their trials. Place both the maror and charoset on the table, ready for use during the meal. These elements remind us that even in the midst of suffering, there is the promise of deliverance, and that our faith can transform even the bitterest experiences into opportunities for growth and hope.

Wine

The wine (or grape juice) used during the Seder is symbolic of the four expressions of deliverance found in Exodus 6:6-7: "I will bring you out," "I will deliver you," "I will redeem you," and "I will take you to me for a people." Ensure that there is enough wine or juice for each participant to have four cups throughout the meal, as these will be poured and drunk at specific points during the Seder.

These four cups represent the stages of God's redemption and our response to His saving acts. Each cup is a moment of reflection and thanksgiving, inviting us to consider the ways in which God has delivered us in our own lives and continues to call us into deeper relationship with Him.

The Washing of the Feet

One of the most significant moments in the Christian Seder is the washing of the feet, a gesture that reflects Jesus' actions at the Last Supper. This act of humility and service is a powerful reminder of Christ's love and the example He set for us. Prepare a basin of water, a jug, and a towel for this purpose, placing them in a central location where they can be easily accessed when it's time to perform the washing.

The washing of the feet is more than a symbolic act; it is an invitation to embody the love and service that Jesus demonstrated. As you prepare for this ritual, reflect on what it means to serve others in humility and how this act can deepen your connection to the community gathered around the table.

Preparing the Meal

The meal itself is an essential part of the Seder, and it should be prepared with the same care and attention as the symbolic elements. Traditionally, lamb is served to recall the Passover lamb sacrificed in Egypt. However, other dishes may be included depending on your tradition, with the meal also featuring the matzah, maror, charoset, and other symbolic foods that have been prepared.

This meal is more than sustenance; it is a tangible connection to the Exodus story and a celebration of God's provision. As you prepare the meal, consider how each dish reflects the themes of sacrifice, redemption, and community that are central to the Seder.

Additional Items

Consider preparing small bowls of water at each place setting for hand washing (Urchatz and Rachtzah). This act of purification is an important part of the Seder, symbolizing the need to cleanse ourselves as we enter into this sacred story. The physical act of washing our hands serves as a reminder that approaching God requires both an inward and outward preparation.

Final Preparations

As you complete the ritual preparations, take a moment to pause and reflect on the significance of each item and action. The Seder is more than a meal; it is an invitation to participate in the ongoing story of God's deliverance. The time and care you invest in these preparations set the stage for a meaningful and spiritually enriching experience, one that connects the ancient traditions of our faith with the living reality of God's presence in our lives today.

By preparing each element with intention, you create a space where the story of the Exodus can be experienced anew, where the past and present converge in a powerful act of remembrance and hope.

Setting the Table

Now that the ritual elements are prepared, it's time to set the Seder table, creating a space that invites all participants into a sacred encounter. The setting of the table is not just about arranging items; it's about establishing an atmosphere where the divine story of redemption can unfold. Each item on the table plays a crucial role in the narrative, and how they are arranged helps to tell this story.

Creating a Sacred Space

As you begin to set the table, focus on creating a space that feels sacred and inviting. The table should be covered with a simple white cloth, symbolizing purity and new beginnings. Place at least two candles at the center of the table; these will be lit at the beginning of the Seder to represent the light of God's presence, marking the transition from the ordinary to the sacred.

For Each Person, Prepare:

- **Glass for Wine (or Grape Juice)**: Ensure each setting includes a glass, with enough wine or juice for four cups per person, as these will be poured at specific moments during the meal.

- **Glass for Water**: Provide an additional glass for water at each setting, with bottles or jars of water placed on the table for drinking throughout the meal.

- **Matzah (Unleavened Bread)**: Plan for about one piece of matzah per person, with three pieces set aside on the Seder plate. This bread is a powerful reminder of the haste with which the Israelites left Egypt.

- **Small Dish for Dipping**: Include a small dish at each place setting for dipping the vegetable (karpas) into salt water.

- **Cutlery and Tableware:** Ensure there is enough cutlery for all participants, including forks, knives, and spoons, especially for carving and eating the lamb. Plates and bowls should also be placed for both the symbolic foods and the meal itself.
- **An extra wine glass for Elijah the Prophet.**

Arranging the Symbolic Foods

Once the essentials are in place, you can arrange the additional symbolic foods that have been prepared. These foods are not just items on the table; they are powerful symbols that tell the story of the Exodus and God's deliverance.

- **Karpas (Vegetable):** Fresh parsley or other greens should be placed in a small dish on the table, along with a bowl of salt water nearby. This will be dipped in the salt water early in the Seder, symbolizing the tears shed by the Israelites during their slavery.
- **Maror (Bitter Herbs):** Horseradish, prepared earlier, symbolizes the harshness of slavery and should be placed on the table for everyone to partake during the meal.
- **Charoset:** This sweet mixture, representing the mortar used by the Israelites, also reflects the hope of redemption. Place a dish of charoset on the table, ready for use later in the meal.

- **Roasted Lamb Shank**: Represents the Passover lamb that was sacrificed, symbolizing God's deliverance of His people. If your group is large, consider bringing the entire roasted lamb to the table. This not only enhances the communal experience but also vividly recalls the sacrificial lamb of the Passover.

- **Roasted Egg**: Symbolizes life, fertility, and the connection to the Passover sacrifice.

Final Preparations and Spiritual Atmosphere

With the table nearly ready, the final touches are crucial to creating the right spiritual atmosphere. These elements help to set the tone and prepare everyone for a meaningful Seder experience.

- **Lighting the Candles**: Begin the Seder by lighting the candles, accompanied by a blessing that thanks God for the gift of light and the holiness of the occasion. This act marks the transition from the ordinary to the sacred.

- **Opening Prayers**: Start the meal with a prayer or moment of silence to center everyone's hearts on the significance of the Seder.

- **Music and Readings**: Consider incorporating soft background music or Scripture readings that reflect themes of deliverance, sacrifice, and redemption. These elements help to enhance the reflective nature of the Seder, inviting participants to enter into a deeper contemplation of God's saving work.

- **Head Coverings:** In some traditions, participants wear head coverings (kippahs) during the Seder as a sign of reverence.

- **Preparation of the Environment:** Ensure the table is arranged in a way that encourages a sense of sacred unity. The smells of roasted lamb, herbs, and charoset should fill the air, enhancing the sensory experience.

With these preparations in place, the Seder table is not just set—it is ready to host a sacred encounter with God. Every detail, from the symbolic foods to the candles and water glasses, plays a part in telling the story of God's deliverance. As you gather around the table, remember that you are participating in an ancient tradition that connects you to the ongoing story of God's faithful love and redemption.

The Dynamics and Roles

Before we get into the spiritual atmosphere of the Seder, it's important to understand the roles and dynamics that help guide this special meal. The Seder is more than just a ritual; it's a family gathering where everyone plays an important part in bringing the story of God's deliverance to life. By assigning these roles, we make sure that everyone is involved, allowing the evening to flow with purpose and meaning. For Christians, the Seder also holds deeper significance, as it reflects the fulfillment of God's promises in Jesus.

The Role of the Father (The Leader)

The father usually leads the Seder, similar to how God leads His people. As the head of the household, the father guides the family through the different parts of the meal, leading prayers, reading scriptures, and breaking the matzah. These actions aren't just about following tradition; they are acts of spiritual leadership that help build the faith of the entire family.

In the Bible, the father's role in the Seder echoes how Moses led the Israelites during the first Passover, following God's command to remember this event every year. For Christians, this role is even more meaningful. The father, as the leader, represents Christ, who led His disciples through the Last Supper and gave us the Eucharist. By leading the Seder, the father is not only remembering the Exodus but also pointing to Jesus, who freed us from sin through His sacrifice.

When the father leads the Seder, he's not just telling a story from the past; he's helping the family see themselves as part of God's ongoing work of salvation. His role is to remind everyone that they are God's people, saved not just from physical hardship, but from sin, thanks to Jesus.

The Role of the Mother

While the father leads, the mother's role is just as important, even if it's sometimes quieter. Traditionally, the mother starts the Seder by lighting the candles, which marks the beginning of sacred time. This act symbolizes the light and warmth she brings to the home, making it a place where God's presence can be felt.

In Christian thought, the mother's role can be seen as reflecting the Church—Christ's Bride—who prepares believers to receive Christ, the light of the world. Just as the Church nurtures and supports our faith, the mother's care and preparation create an environment where God's love is experienced. Her role during the Seder reminds us that this meal isn't just a ritual but a meaningful experience, carefully prepared and shared with love.

Throughout the Seder, the mother ensures that everything is ready and in its place. This reflects how God cares for us and prepares us to receive His grace. Her role is like the Holy Spirit, quietly preparing our hearts and minds to enter into the sacredness of the Seder.

The Role of the Children

Children have a special place at the Seder table because they represent the future of faith and the continuation of tradition. The Seder is designed to spark their curiosity and teach them about God's deliverance in a way that is both engaging and memorable. The youngest child traditionally asks the Four Questions, which is a key moment in the Seder that highlights the importance of passing down faith to the next generation.

This role is rooted in the Bible, where God instructed the Israelites to teach their children about the Exodus (Exodus 13:8). For Christians, this role also reminds us of Jesus' teaching that we must become like little children to enter the Kingdom of Heaven (Matthew 18:3). The children's involvement in the Seder helps them begin their own journey of faith, learning about their heritage and about the God who is still active in their lives today.

The Seder is not just about teaching; it's about shaping the faith of the next generation. By participating, children are drawn into the story of God's faithfulness, forming their own relationship with Him and understanding their place in His ongoing story.

The Role of All Participants

While the father, mother, and children each have specific roles, the Seder is a communal experience where everyone plays a part. Whether by reading, singing, or simply sharing in the meal, each person helps bring the story of God's deliverance to life. The Seder is a living tradition, a shared act of remembrance and celebration that unites everyone in God's story.

For Christians, this communal aspect is particularly meaningful, as it mirrors the unity of the Body of Christ. Just as the early Christians gathered to break bread and share in the Eucharist, the Seder brings people together to remember God's mighty works and look forward to the fulfillment of His Kingdom. Participating in the Seder together is a way to strengthen our bonds of faith, hope, and love as we remember what Christ has done for us and look forward to His return.

As you prepare for the Seder, think about the importance of these roles. Each person at the table is an essential part of the story of God's redemption, a story that began with the Exodus and finds its fulfillment in the life, death, and resurrection of Jesus Christ. By participating, the Seder becomes more than a meal; it becomes a living encounter with the God who saves, redeems, and continues to work in our lives today.

The Spiritual Atmosphere

With roles clearly defined, we can now turn our attention to cultivating the spiritual atmosphere of the Seder. This isn't just about the physical setting; it's about preparing our hearts and minds to enter into a sacred space where we can encounter the living God. The environment we create will help set the tone for the evening, transforming the meal from a simple gathering into a profound spiritual experience that draws each participant closer to God.

Lighting the Candles

We begin by lighting the candles, an act rich in symbolism. The flickering flames represent the light of God's presence, reminding us of His guidance throughout history and His continued presence in our lives. As it is written in the Psalms, "Your word is a lamp to my feet and a light to my path" (Psalm 119:105). The lighting of the candles signifies our transition from the ordinary routines of life into a time of holy reflection and communion with God.

Opening Prayer and Silence

Following the lighting of the candles, we pause for a moment of silence or an opening prayer. This moment is an invitation for the Holy Spirit to fill the space and our hearts, much like the disciples who gathered in the Upper Room waiting for the promise of the Spirit. Jesus assured them, "Where two or three are gathered in my name, I am there among them" (Matthew 18:20). As we gather for the Seder, we too invite His presence, asking the Spirit to guide our thoughts, soften our hearts, and open our eyes to the deep truths we will explore.

Scripture Readings

To further deepen this spiritual atmosphere, consider incorporating Scripture readings that resonate with the themes of deliverance, sacrifice, and redemption. The Psalms of Hallel (Psalms 113-118) are traditionally recited during the Passover meal, each verse echoing the faithfulness of God and His mighty acts of salvation. As Psalm 118:14-15 declares, "The Lord is my strength and my might; He has become my salvation. There are glad songs of victory in the tents of the righteous." These Psalms not only recall God's past deliverance but also point forward to the ultimate salvation offered through Christ.

Music

Music also plays a powerful role in shaping the spiritual atmosphere. Soft, instrumental music can create a background that encourages reflection and prayer. Alternatively, singing hymns or spiritual songs can lift the hearts of all present, uniting them in worship and praise.

Colossians 3:16 reminds us, "Let the word of Christ dwell in you richly; teach and admonish one another in all wisdom; and with gratitude in your hearts sing psalms, hymns, and spiritual songs to God." This music is not mere decoration; it is a means of drawing nearer to God, of expressing our gratitude, and of opening ourselves to the movement of the Spirit.

Active Participation

As we continue through the Seder, it's essential to maintain an attitude of active, prayerful participation. The Seder is not just a meal; it's an act of worship, a retelling of the story of God's deliverance. Encourage each participant to engage fully, whether through reading, singing, or sharing personal reflections.

This communal participation transforms the Seder from a passive experience into a dynamic encounter with God's redemptive story. In sharing our thoughts and insights, we fulfill the commandment to "teach them to your children, talking about them when you sit at home and when you walk along the road, when you lie down and when you get up" (Deuteronomy 11:19).

Preparing Hearts for Encounter

Ultimately, creating a spiritual atmosphere is about more than just the physical environment; it's about preparing our hearts to meet with God. The Seder is an invitation to step into the sacred story of salvation, to remember God's faithfulness, and to renew our commitment to walk in His ways. As we light the candles, offer prayers, read Scripture, and sing songs, let us do so with hearts full of reverence, gratitude, and expectation, trusting that God will meet us in this sacred moment.

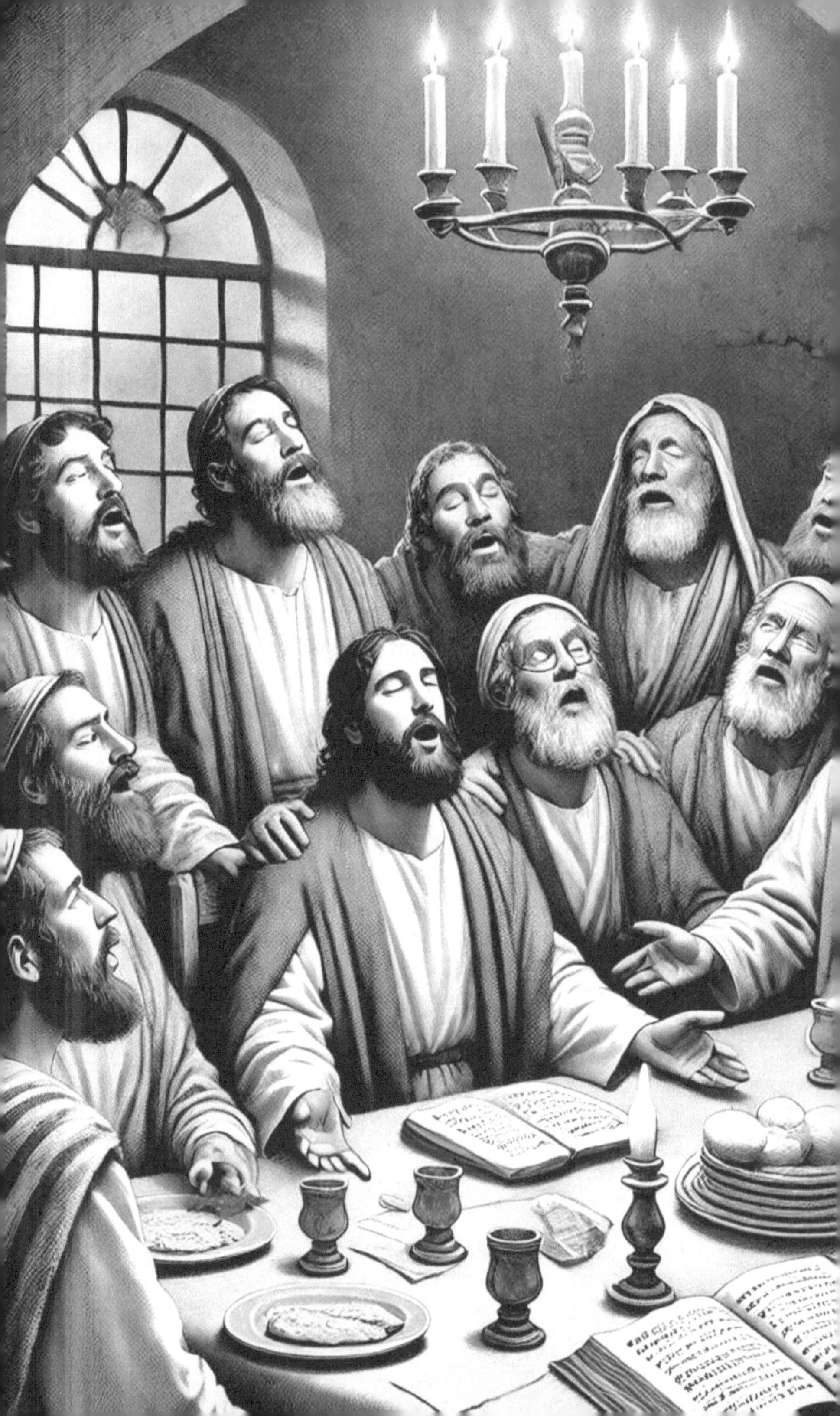

PART 4

THE SEDER RITE

This section of the book presents the full rite of the Seder meal, a tradition rich in symbolism and deeply rooted in the history of God's deliverance. Before beginning the Seder, it's crucial to prepare both practically and spiritually. This introduction will help you assign roles and make sure everything is in place for a meaningful and spiritually enriching celebration.

Instructions and Roles

- **Father (Presider):** The main leader who guides the Seder, recites key passages, and performs significant actions like breaking the bread and lifting the cups.

- **Mother:** Traditionally assists in serving the meal and may also participate in specific readings or blessings, symbolizing her integral role in the family's spiritual life.

- **Youngest Child:** Asks the Four Questions during the Seder, symbolizing curiosity and the passing of tradition to the next generation.

- **Commentator:** Provides explanations, introduces readings, and leads the group in reflections or songs.

- **Readers:** Different participants can be assigned to read specific passages, including the Ten Commandments and Psalms.

Checklist for the Seder Meal

- **Seder Plate:** Includes symbolic foods like matzah (unleavened bread), maror (bitter herbs), charoset (sweet mixture), and a roasted lamb shank.
- **Candles:** For the lighting ceremony at the beginning of the Seder.
- **Wine or Grape Juice:** Four cups per person, symbolizing different stages of God's promise and deliverance.
- **Fresh Herbs (Karpas):** Often parsley, symbolizing new life.
- **Salt Water:** Represents the tears shed during slavery in Egypt.
- **Matzah (Unleavened Bread):** For the blessings and to be eaten during the meal.
- **Bitter Herb Sauce (Maror):** For dipping the matzah and herbs.
- **Charoset:** A sweet mixture of apples, nuts, and wine, symbolizing the mortar used by the Israelites in building.
- **Roasted Egg:** Symbolizes life and fertility, connected to the Passover sacrifice.
- **Lamb:** Represents the Passover lamb that was sacrificed, commemorating God's deliverance.

As you prepare to lead or participate in the Seder, it's important to **approach this time with reverence, calmness, and a spirit of flexibility**. While the structure of the Seder is guided by tradition, there is room to adapt certain elements to fit the needs of your family or group. For example, the Four Questions, traditionally asked by the youngest child, can be divided among several children to involve them all in this sacred moment. This not only keeps the children engaged but also emphasizes the communal nature of the Seder, where everyone has a role in the telling of the Exodus story.

Creating an atmosphere of calm and reverence is key to a meaningful experience. **Encourage participants to take their time with each part of the meal**, allowing space for reflection and prayer. The Seder is not just a retelling of history; it is an invitation to enter into the story of God's deliverance, to see ourselves as part of this ongoing narrative of redemption. As you move through each step of the Seder, from the lighting of the candles to the breaking of the matzah, allow the symbols and actions to speak deeply to your heart and the hearts of those gathered.

Flexibility is also important. If you sense that a particular part of the Seder is resonating with the group, don't rush through it. Allow time for additional discussion, reflection, or even a spontaneous prayer. The Seder is meant to be a living tradition, one that adapts to the needs and dynamics of those who participate. Whether it's assigning different readings to various family members, choosing songs that are meaningful to your group, or simply taking a moment of silence to let the significance of the meal sink in, remember that the ultimate goal is to draw closer to God and to one another.

This section of the book provides the full rite of the Seder meal. As you enter into this sacred journey, may you find that each role, each symbol, and each word spoken brings you closer to the heart of God's redemptive love. Let this time be one of deep spiritual enrichment, where the ancient traditions of Passover come alive in your own context, renewing your faith and drawing you into a deeper relationship with God.

With everything prepared, you are now ready to enter into the sacred time of the Seder. May this meal be a profound encounter with the God who delivers, redeems, and continues to work in the lives of His people today.

BEGINNING THE SEDER

Commentator: Welcome to this special Seder meal. Tonight, we are about to embark on a journey that connects us with the roots of our faith and the history of God's people. The Seder is a traditional meal celebrated by our Jewish brothers and sisters to remember the Exodus from Egypt—God's deliverance of the Israelites from slavery.

However, tonight's Seder is different. As Christians, we are incorporating Christ's Last Supper into this tradition, helping us understand how Jesus established the Eucharist. This allows us to see how He fulfilled the Old Testament promises and brought us into a new covenant with God.

Each of you will have a role to play, just as in the original Passover celebration. These roles and the symbolic foods we'll encounter have deep meanings, which will be explained as we go. The Seder is more than a meal; it's a way to remember and relive the story of God's deliverance—from Egypt and from sin through Christ.

As we proceed, you'll discover the profound love God has for His people through the elements of this meal, like the matzah, bitter herbs, and wine. Each tells part of the story, both of the Exodus and Christ's ultimate sacrifice.

Let's begin with open hearts, ready to experience the Seder in a way that honors our shared heritage with the Jewish people and the new life we have in Christ. This is a time of reflection, learning, and celebration. The rite will explain itself as we go along, and by the end of the evening, you'll have a deeper understanding of both the roots of our faith and the gift of the Eucharist.

Before we begin, we'll read a passage from the Gospel of Mark (Mark 14:12-16), where Jesus sends His disciples to prepare for the Passover meal. This passage will be read by our leader, traditionally called the Father, setting the stage for our Seder.

The Father (or Leader):

A reading from the Holy Gospel according to Mark.

On the first day of Unleavened Bread, when the Passover lamb is sacrificed, His disciples said to Him, 'Where do you want us to go and make the preparations for you to eat the Passover?' So He sent two of His disciples, saying to them, 'Go into the city, and a man carrying a jar of water will meet you; follow him, and wherever he enters, say to the owner of the house, "The Teacher asks, Where is my guest room where I may eat the Passover with my disciples?" He will show you a large room upstairs, furnished and ready. Make preparations for us there.' So the disciples set out and went to the city and found everything as He had told them; and they prepared the Passover meal.

The Word of the Lord.

All: Thanks be to God

Commentator: Now, let us listen to the Father, who will guide us into this time of remembrance and thanksgiving.

The Father: United with our Jewish brothers and sisters, tonight we celebrate the long history of the Jewish people—a history of spiritual struggles and the pursuit of justice and freedom. We give thanks to the Eternal One for sustaining us through every trial, and for the Exodus from Egypt, the light of God's law, and the dignity established by the Ten Commandments, Torah, and Sabbath.

But tonight, we also remember that this sacred history finds its fulfillment in Christ, the true Passover Lamb. Just as our ancestors were delivered from slavery in Egypt, so too have we been delivered from sin and death through Christ's sacrifice. Let us give thanks for this deliverance and prepare our hearts to enter this sacred time, mindful of God's great works in our lives.

Opening Prayer

The Father (or Leader): Let us now take a moment to quiet our hearts and minds as we prepare to enter into this sacred time. We are here to recall the story of God's deliverance, to reflect on His faithfulness, and to renew our commitment to living as His people.

A silent pause is observed, and then, led by the Father, all say the following prayer together.

All: Blessed are You, Lord our God, King of the universe, who has kept us alive, sustained us, and brought us to this season. As we begin this Seder, we ask for Your blessing upon our gathering. May our hearts be open to the lessons of this evening, and may our minds be focused on the meaning behind the symbols before us.

The Father: We now take a moment to acknowledge the symbols on our Seder table, each representing a part of the story we are about to recount. These symbols remind us of the journey from slavery to freedom and of the hope we have in God's promises. Let's read the meaning of each item together:

All:

- **Matzah (Unleavened Bread):** The bread of affliction, reminding us of the rush with which our ancestors left Egypt.

- **Maror (Bitter Herbs):** A symbol of the bitterness of slavery that the Israelites endured.

- **Charoset:** A sweet mixture representing the mortar the Israelites used during their forced labor, reminding us of their hardship and hope.

- **Karpas (Fresh Herbs):** A sign of new life and hope, dipped in salt water to recall the tears shed in slavery.

- **Salt Water:** A reminder of the tears and suffering endured by the Israelites.

- **Zeroa (Shank Bone):** Symbolizes the Passover lamb, whose blood spared the Israelites during the final plague.

- **Beitzah (Roasted Egg):** Represents the cycle of life and renewal, and the offerings once brought to the Temple.

- **Wine:** Signifies the four promises of redemption that God made in Exodus, namely: "I will bring you out," "I will deliver you," "I will redeem you," and "I will take you to be My people."

The Father: These symbols remind us of God's past deliverance and His ongoing promises. As we proceed with our Seder, let these symbols guide us, reflecting on our ancestors' struggles and God's faithfulness. With our hearts and minds centered on the significance of this evening, we now move to the lighting of the candles, marking the transition from ordinary time to sacred time, and inviting the light of God's presence among us.

Pause to allow the lighting of the candles.

The Father: Let us now prayer together:

All: Blessed are You, Lord our God, King of the universe, who has made us holy with His commandments and commanded us to light the festival lights.

A Song of Praise

The Father: With the candles lit, our hearts are now prepared to enter into the ancient story of God's deliverance. We turn our focus to the Hallel, a series of Psalms (113 through 118) sung during significant Jewish festivals, including Passover. These Psalms are expressions of praise and gratitude for God's mighty acts of salvation. As we recite them tonight, we join countless generations in celebrating God's faithfulness, power, and enduring love.

Traditionally, the Hallel is recited in two parts during the Seder. The first part, Psalm 113, is sung before the meal, recalling the Exodus from Egypt. The second part, Psalms 114 to 118, is recited after the meal, reflecting on God's continued deliverance and the hope for future redemption.

Let us sing these Psalms together, responsively, echoing the ancient tradition. As we lift our voices in praise, may we remember the great works God has done and continues to do in our lives. His promises are true, and His love endures forever.

Please remain seated as we recite the Hallel Psalms.

Psalm 113

God the Helper of the Needy

Praise the Lord!
Praise, O servants of the Lord;
 praise the name of the Lord.

Blessed be the name of the Lord
 from this time on and forevermore.
From the rising of the sun to its setting,
 the name of the Lord is to be praised.
The Lord is high above all nations
 and his glory above the heavens.

Who is like the Lord our God,
 who is seated on high,
who looks far down
 on the heavens and the earth?
He raises the poor from the dust
 and lifts the needy from the ash heap,
to make them sit with princes,
 with the princes of his people.
He gives the barren woman a home,
 making her the joyous mother of children.
Praise the Lord!

Blessing and First Cup

The Father: As we move into the celebration of the Seder, we begin with the sanctification of this special day, known as the Kadesh. This part of the Seder is where we recognize the holiness of this moment and prepare ourselves to enter fully into the story of God's deliverance.

The Father then lifts the first cup of wine, while everyone remains seated.

The Father: We start by lifting the first cup of wine, which represents joy and freedom. This first cup, known as the Cup of Sanctification, reminds us of God's promise to bring the Israelites out from under the burdens of the Egyptians. It symbolizes our separation from what enslaves us and our commitment to entering into the sacred story of God's deliverance.

Let us now offer a blessing over this first cup.

All: Blessed are You, Lord our God, King of the universe, who has chosen us from among all peoples, lifting us above all languages, and sanctified us with Your commandments. With great love, O Lord our God, You have given us times of joy, seasons of gladness, and this festival of Unleavened Bread, the season of our freedom, a holy convocation, a memorial of the Exodus from Egypt. For You have chosen us and sanctified us from among all the nations. In Your love, You have given us Your holy festivals as an inheritance for rejoicing and for sanctifying. Blessed are You, Lord, who sanctifies Israel and the festive seasons.

The Father: Before drinking each cup of wine, we say a blessing over the wine.

All participants, while seated and with heads covered, lift their cups of wine.

All: Blessed are You, Lord our God, King of the universe, Creator of the fruit of the vine.

The Father: And now, we say the blessing that reminds us that this life is but a passage to another, the blessing for the wondrous gift of life, the Shehecheyanu.

All: Blessed are You, Lord our God, King of the universe, who has given us life, sustained us, and brought us to this moment.

Everyone drinks the first cup of wine while reclining to the left, as a symbol of freedom, with heads still covered.

After drinking the wine, participants may remove their head coverings.

WASHING OF THE FEET

The Father: As we continue our Seder, we come to a significant moment of humility and service—the washing of the feet. In the time of Jesus, it was customary to wash the feet of guests as they arrived, a gesture of hospitality and care. The roads were dusty, and sandals offered little protection, so this act was both necessary and refreshing.

During the Last Supper, Jesus added profound meaning to this tradition by washing the feet of His disciples, showing that true greatness in the Kingdom of God is found in serving others, not in being served.

For those who are able, I will now wash the feet of the participants, as Jesus did for His disciples. If washing the feet is not practical for some, washing of the hands is also an appropriate alternative.

The Father stands and puts on the apron to wash the feet (or hands) of those present. When he is ready, he proceeds by saying the following words.

The Father: From the earliest times, we have been instructed to cleanse ourselves before partaking of the provisions of the One who has always been, blessed be His name. It is our tradition to welcome the stranger among us and, as a sign of hospitality, to wash their feet, so they may be refreshed from the heat and cleansed from the dust of the road. Let us bless the name of Him who has cleansed us from all defilement.

All participants cover their heads for the blessing.

All Together: Blessed are You, Lord our God, Creator of all, who sanctifies us with Your holy days and commands us to be cleansed so that we may appear clean before You.

The Father now proceeds with the washing of feet or hands.

As the washing of feet or hands takes place, soft background music may be played. While the Father begins washing the feet or hands, one of the participants can read the passage commemorating the episode where Jesus washed the feet of His disciples. This reading can be done while soft background music is being played.

After the reading of the Gospel, traditional Gregorian chant or reflective hymns, such as "Ubi Caritas," "The Servant Song," or "Pange Lingua," can deepen the spiritual atmosphere, allowing participants to enter more fully into this act of service and humility. This is a time for quiet reflection on the example of Jesus and how we are called to serve one another with love and humility.

A Reading from the Gospel of Saint John

Before the festival of the Passover, Jesus knew that his hour had come to depart from this world and go to the Father. Having loved his own who were in the world, he loved them to the end. The devil had already put it into the heart of Judas son of Simon Iscariot to betray him. And during supper Jesus, knowing that the Father had given all things into his hands, and that he had come from God and was going to God, got up from the table, took off his outer robe, and tied a towel around himself. Then he poured water into a basin and began to wash the disciples' feet and to wipe them with the towel that was tied around him. He came to Simon Peter, who said to him, "Lord, are you going to wash my feet?" Jesus answered, "You do not know now what I am doing, but later you will understand." Peter said to him, "You will never wash my feet."

Jesus answered, "Unless I wash you, you have no share with me." Simon Peter said to him, "Lord, not my feet only but also my hands and my head!" Jesus said to him, "One who has bathed does not need to wash, except for the feet, but is entirely clean. And you are clean, though not all of you." For he knew who was to betray him; for this reason, he said, "Not all of you are clean."

After he had washed their feet, had put on his robe, and had returned to the table, he said to them, "Do you know what I have done to you? You call me Teacher and Lord—and you are right, for that is what I am. So if I, your Lord and Teacher, have washed your feet, you also ought to wash one another's feet. For I have set you an example, that you also should do as I have done to you. Very truly, I tell you, servants are not greater than their master, nor are messengers greater than the one who sent them. If you know these things, you are blessed if you do them. I am not speaking of all of you; I know whom I have chosen. But it is to fulfill the scripture, 'The one who ate my bread has lifted his heel against me.' I tell you this now, before it occurs, so that when it does occur, you may believe that I am he. Very truly, I tell you, whoever receives one whom I send receives me; and whoever receives me receives him who sent me."

The Word of the Lord.
Thanks be to God.

Breaking of the Matzah

The Father: We now come to an important moment in our Seder—the breaking of the middle matzah, called Yachatz. This unleavened bread reminds us of the bread of affliction that our ancestors ate in Egypt and the haste with which they left, with no time for the dough to rise.

I will now break the middle matzah into two pieces. The smaller piece will be returned to the plate, and the larger piece, known as the Afikoman, will be set aside and hidden to be eaten later as the final part of our meal.

This act symbolizes the brokenness in our lives and our world, but it also introduces a sense of hope and anticipation. Just as we will later find the Afikoman and bring it back, we hold onto the hope that what is broken will one day be made whole through God's grace.

The Father breaks the middle matzah, returns the smaller piece to the Seder plate, and sets aside the larger piece as the Afikoman, to be hidden for later.

The Renewal of All Creation – Spring

The Father: As we continue our Seder, we now come to a moment that celebrates the renewal of all creation. In this part of the meal, we reflect on the new life that comes with spring—a symbol of hope and rebirth that our ancestors cherished as they awaited their deliverance from Egypt. For us as Christians, this renewal is also a reminder of the new life we have through Christ's resurrection.

Let us take a moment to remember the plants of the earth and the salt of the sea, which come together to sustain life. In the midst of slavery, our ancestors found strength in the hope that life would be renewed, just as the earth is renewed each spring.

We hear these beautiful words from the Song of Songs, reminding us of the renewal that God brings:

"For now the winter is past,
the rain is over and gone.
The flowers appear on the earth;
the time of singing has come,
and the voice of the turtledove
is heard in our land.
The fig tree puts forth its figs,
and the vines are in blossom;

they give forth fragrance."
(Song of Solomon 2:11-13)

Just as the earth is renewed each spring, so too are we renewed through God's grace and deliverance. In Christ, we see the ultimate fulfillment of this renewal, as He brings new life to all who believe.

All Together: Blessed are You, Lord our God, King of the universe, Creator of the fruit of the earth.

The Father: We now dip the herbs into the salt water, remembering the tears of our ancestors and the new life that comes through God's deliverance. As we eat these herbs, let us reflect on the bitterness of suffering and the sweetness of the hope we have in Christ, who has conquered death and offers us eternal life.

All participants dip the herbs into the salt water, eat them, and continue the Seder.

The Story of the Exodus

The Father: Now, we recall the story of our ancestors, a story of deliverance that echoes through time, finding its ultimate fulfillment in Christ. Let us recount the mighty works of God, who brought our forefathers out of Egypt and who, through Jesus, brings us out of the bondage of sin..

All: This is the bread of affliction that our ancestors ate in the land of Egypt. Let all who are hungry come and eat; let all who are in need come and share in the Passover with us. This year we are here; next year, may we be in the land of Israel. This year we are still slaves; next year, may we be free.

The Father then places the smaller piece of the broken middle matzah, which was set aside earlier, back on the Seder plate with the other matzot.

This action signifies the continuation of our Seder, preparing us to bless and partake of the matzah as we proceed with the meal.

The Father: Even the youngest among us can see the unleavened bread on the Seder table. This is the bread without yeast. My child, the youngest here, please ask the four questions that make this night different from all other nights.

The youngest child stands and asks the questions.

The Youngest Child:

1. Father (Abba), why is this night different from all other nights?

2. Why, on all other nights, do we eat leavened bread or matzah, but tonight we eat only matzah?

3. Why, on all other nights, do we eat all kinds of vegetables, but tonight we eat only bitter herbs?

4. Why, on all other nights, we do not dip our food even once, but tonight we dip twice?

5. I wish also to ask you, Why, on all other nights do we eat sitting upright, but tonight we eat while reclining comfortably?

The traditional *Ma Nishtana* (The Four Questions) consists of the first four questions. The fifth question, about sitting upright versus reclining, is sometimes added in some traditions to highlight the fact that they are now free people.

The Father: My child, we were slaves in Egypt. The Eternal, our God, brought us out from there with a mighty hand and an outstretched arm.

All: Because we were slaves to Pharaoh in Egypt, and the Eternal, our God, brought us out from there with a mighty hand and an outstretched arm.

The Mother: Had the Holy One, blessed be His name forever, not brought our ancestors out of Egypt, we, our children, and our children's children would still be enslaved in Egypt.

The Father: We have now heard the four questions, and there are four types of children who might ask them: the one who is indifferent, the simple one, the one who doesn't know how to ask, and the wise one. The indifferent child asks as if he is not one of us, as if he has no part in our story. The simple child asks only what has happened without seeking its meaning. The one who doesn't know how to ask doesn't even consider questioning, thinking there's no need. But my wise child asks and wants to understand the meaning of everything we do.

All: So let us be wise children. Everything we do tonight during this meal has deep meaning for us. Even if we were full of wisdom, respected for our knowledge, or teachers of the Torah, it would still be right to retell the story of our exodus from Egypt and reflect on the meaning of every word.

The Father designates participants to answer the questions. Those chosen to read stand.

Reader 1: You asked why this night is different from all other nights. "Avadim Hayinu"—we were slaves in the land of Egypt. Our ancestors suffered greatly, but tonight we remember how God set us free with a mighty hand and an outstretched arm.

Reader 2: You asked why we eat only matzah (unleavened bread) on this night. "Avadim Hayinu"—we were slaves in the land of Egypt. Our ancestors, when escaping from their bondage in Egypt, didn't have time to let the dough rise, so they baked flat, unleavened bread called matzah. The Holy Scriptures tell us, "We were driven out of Egypt." They couldn't delay; they had no time to prepare food. To remember this, tonight, we eat matzah.

Reader 3: You asked why we eat bitter herbs on this night. "Avadim Hayinu"—we were slaves in the land of Egypt. Today we eat bitter herbs because the Egyptians made our ancestors' lives bitter. The Holy Scriptures declare, "They made their lives bitter with hard labor in mortar and bricks and with all kinds of work in the fields." Their bondage was harsh.

Reader 4: You asked why we dip twice on this night. "Avadim Hayinu"—we were slaves in the land of Egypt. The first time we dip, it is to taste the saltwater, reminding us of the tears of slavery. But now, we also dip to remember the life and fertility of the land and sea, united under God's mercy, which gives us breath to live. The second dipping, in the charoset, recalls the mortar our ancestors used as slaves for Pharaoh in Egypt. But our charoset, a mixture of sweet apples, nuts, and wine, symbolizes the sweetness of freedom our ancestors hoped for even in the bitterness of their slavery.

Reader 5: You asked why we recline comfortably while eating on this night. "Avadim Hayinu"—we were slaves in the land of Egypt. Tonight, we recline comfortably to remember that, like our ancestors, we too can overcome slavery and break every chain, for each of us is a servant to himself, and each of us is free to become his own master.

*The Father stands,
holding the roasted egg from the Seder plate,
and speaks.*

The Father: After escaping Egypt, the Jews arrived in the Promised Land and built the Temple in Jerusalem. There, they brought offerings of thanksgiving for the fruitfulness of the land and the bounty of their flocks. This egg reminds us of life, growth, and the blessing of fertility.

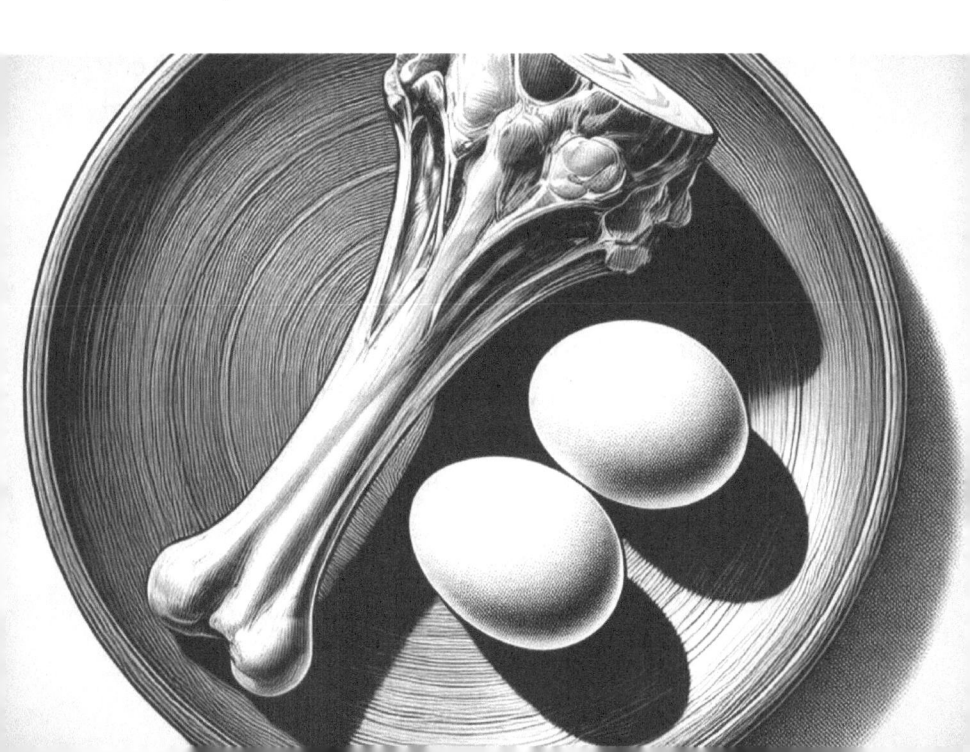

*The Father
lifts the roasted lamb shank and continues.*

The Father: This shank bone reminds us of the Passover lamb, which the Holy One, blessed be His name, commanded the Israelites in Egypt to sacrifice. They were to mark their doorposts with its blood as a sign for the destroying angel to pass over their homes, sparing them while striking down the Egyptians, so their master, Pharaoh, would let our people go, freeing them from their bondage. Let us now ask ourselves: Why were we made slaves in Egypt?

*The Father assigns someone
to retell the story of the Exodus.
Standing as they read.*

Reader 1: The Holy Scriptures tell us that in ancient times, our ancestors lived across the great river among people who worshipped false gods. In the city of Ur, our father Abram was the first to realize that God is One, eternal and everlasting. To worship God means freedom. But Abram had to flee the land of those who worshipped other gods.

Reader 2: The Holy Scriptures say, "I took your father Abram from beyond the river and led him through the land of Canaan." They also say, "And the Lord said to Abram, 'To your offspring, I will give this land, from the river of Egypt to the great river, the Euphrates.'"

Reader 3: The flocks of Abram grew large in the land, and God gave him Isaac. Isaac's son, Jacob, fathered many children, but his favorite was Joseph, who was sold by his jealous brothers to a caravan of Ishmaelites, who took Joseph with them to Egypt.

Reader 4: Joseph rose to become a minister to Pharaoh over all of Egypt. He filled the storehouses with grain, and when famine struck the land, Joseph's brothers came to Egypt to buy food, bringing their father and families with them. In Egypt, the Jews lived and prospered.

Reader 5: But a new king arose in Egypt who did not know Joseph. He said, "Look, the people of Israel have become too numerous and too strong for us." Fearing they might join an enemy in war, Pharaoh set taskmasters over them to oppress them with forced labor. So, our ancestors built for Pharaoh the great cities of Pithom and Ramses. They became slaves!

Reader 6: To destroy our people, Pharaoh ordered the Hebrew midwives to cast every newborn son into the river.

Reader 7: A woman from the tribe of Levi placed her baby boy in a basket made of reeds and set it among the rushes by the riverbank. The child was found by Pharaoh's daughter, who named him Moses, meaning "drawn out of the water."

Reader 8: The child's sister watched over him and arranged for their mother to nurse him. Thus, Moses was raised among his own people.

Reader 9: When Moses grew up, he saw an Egyptian beating a Hebrew and killed the Egyptian. Fleeing from Pharaoh's wrath, Moses fled to the land of Midian.

Reader 10: One day, while tending the flocks, Moses heard the voice of the Eternal speaking to him from a bush that was burning but not consumed, saying, "I am sending you to Pharaoh to bring my people, the Israelites, out of Egypt."

The Father stands.

The Father: As it is written: "We cried out to the Lord, the God of our ancestors, and the Lord heard our voice and saw our suffering, our toil, and our oppression."

All participants stand.

All: And the Lord brought us out of Egypt with a mighty hand and an outstretched arm, with great terror and with signs and wonders.

The Father: Plague after plague fell upon the Egyptians. Out of sorrow and regret for the evil and suffering in the world, our ancestors and we, as we remember the plagues and their number, let drops of wine fall from our cups as a sign of our joy that the Holy One, blessed be His name, delivered us from them.

All: Let us express our joy for the journey to freedom.

*All participants
let three drops of wine fall onto their plates.*

The Father: And let us recall the ten plagues (curses).

*The plagues are read aloud one by one,
and with each one,
everyone lets a drop of wine fall onto their plate.*

All:

1. The waters of Egypt turned to blood
2. Frogs
3. Gnats
4. Flies
5. Pestilence on livestock
6. Boils
7. Hail
8. Locusts
9. Darkness
10. Death of the firstborn

All participants sit, except for the Father.

The Father: Then, after even Pharaoh's son was struck down and died in the final plague, Pharaoh rose in the night and summoned Moses, commanding him to leave with his people. In great haste, the children of Israel departed, as it is written: they baked their bread quickly, for they could not delay. When they reached the shores of the Sea of Reeds (the Red Sea), Pharaoh changed his mind and sent his chariots after them.

The reader stands.

The Eldest Son: The Lord parted the waters, and the Israelites crossed the sea strong and safe. Then the sea closed again over the Egyptians with all their chariots. Thus, the children of Israel were saved.

The Mother: And just as these ten plagues, there is also an ancient story that tells how the Egyptians drowned. When the Israelites crossed strong and safe, the angels in heaven sang a song of praise to God. But God looked down at the waters, as they closed over the Egyptians, and said: "How can you sing when my children are drowning?"

All participants stand.

All: Let us remember and never forget. We were slaves to Pharaoh in Egypt, and the Eternal, our God, brought us out from there with a mighty hand and an outstretched arm. Had the Holy One, blessed be His name, not brought our ancestors out of Egypt, we, our children, and our children's children would still be slaves in Egypt.

All participants sit, except for the reader.

The Father: Let us remember and never forget. The promise of the Eternal to deliver our people was fulfilled, and it has been fulfilled again and again throughout the ages.

Reader 1: Blessed is the One who kept His promise to Israel. For the Holy One, knowing what would happen, foretold to our father Abram what He would do. He said to Abram: "Know for certain that your descendants will be strangers in a land that is not theirs, and they will be enslaved and oppressed for four hundred years. But I will bring judgment on the nation they serve, and afterward, they will come out with great possessions."

*All participants stand
and lift their second cup of wine.*

The Father: All participants, please stand and lift your second cup of wine. This cup, known as the Cup of Deliverance, represents God's promise to deliver His people from bondage. Though we lift it now in anticipation, we will not drink from it just yet. Instead, we hold it as a sign of our readiness to receive God's deliverance, just as the Israelites awaited their freedom from Egypt.

As we stand together, let us reflect on the significance of this moment. THE CUP OF DELIVERANCE reminds us that God is always at work, leading us from darkness into light, from slavery into freedom. This moment connects us with our ancestors in faith, who also stood on the brink of deliverance, waiting for God's mighty hand to act.

Let us remain standing as we continue with the next part of our Seder, keeping this cup raised as a symbol of our trust in God's unfailing promises.

Reader 2: This is the promise that He kept with our ancestors and with us after them.

All: For it was not just one who rose up against us to destroy us, but in every generation, there are those who seek to annihilate us. Yet the Holy One, blessed be His name, is our Deliverer from their hands.

The Father: In every generation, each of us should regard ourselves as if we personally had come out of Egypt. As it is written: "On that day, you shall tell your child: 'It is because of what the Lord did for me when I came out of Egypt.'"

All participants cover their heads.

All: This is because of what the Eternal did for us when He brought us out of Egypt. When we are bound to give thanks, to praise, to glorify, to exalt, to bless, to honor, and to worship the One who performed all these wonders for our ancestors and for us. He brought us from slavery to freedom, from sorrow to joy, from mourning to a festival, from darkness to light, and from servitude to redemption. Therefore, let us sing a new song before Him. Hallelujah!

Blessed are You, Eternal our God, King of the universe, who has delivered us and our ancestors from Egypt and brought us to this night to eat matzah and bitter herbs. So too, Eternal, our God and God of our ancestors, bring us to future festivals in peace, so that we may rejoice in Your service. There, we will sing a new song for our freedom and the redemption of our souls. Blessed are You, Eternal, who has delivered Israel!

All participants sit and place the cup of wine back on the table.

The Father: These are the Psalms that were sung in the Temple on Passover.

While all remain seated with their heads covered, they recite or sing the following Psalms.

Psalm 114

God's Wonders at the Exodus

When Israel went out from Egypt,
  the house of Jacob from a people
  of strange language,
Judah became God's sanctuary,
  Israel his dominion.

The sea looked and fled;
  Jordan turned back.
The mountains skipped like rams,
  the hills like lambs.

Why is it, O sea, that you flee?
  O Jordan, that you turn back?
O mountains, that you skip like rams?
  O hills, like lambs?

Tremble, O earth, at the presence of the Lord,
  at the presence of the God of Jacob,
who turns the rock into a pool of water,
  the flint into a spring of water.

Psalm 115

The Impotence of Idols and the Greatness of God

Not to us, O Lord, not to us,
    but to your name give glory,
    for the sake of your steadfast love
    and your faithfulness.
Why should the nations say,
    "Where is their God?"

Our God is in the heavens;
    he does whatever he pleases.
Their idols are silver and gold,
    the work of human hands.
They have mouths, but they do not speak;
    they have eyes, but they do not see.
They have ears, but they do not hear;
    they have noses, but they do not smell.
They have hands, but they do not feel;
    they have feet, but they do not walk;
    they make no sound in their throats.
Those who make them are like them;
    so are all who trust in them.

O Israel, trust in the Lord!
    He is their help and their shield.
O house of Aaron, trust in the Lord!
    He is their help and their shield.
You who fear the Lord, trust in the Lord!
    He is their help and their shield.

The Lord has been mindful of us; he will bless us;
   he will bless the house of Israel;
   he will bless the house of Aaron;
he will bless those who fear the Lord,
   both small and great.

May the Lord give you increase,
   both you and your children.
May you be blessed by the Lord,
   who made heaven and earth.

The heavens are the Lord's heavens,
   but the earth he has given to human beings.
The dead do not praise the Lord,
   nor do any who go down into silence.
But we will bless the Lord
   from this time on and forevermore.
Praise the Lord!

Psalm 116

Thanksgiving for Recovery from Illness

I love the Lord because he has heard
    my voice and my supplications.
Because he inclined his ear to me,
    therefore I will call on him as long as I live.
The snares of death encompassed me;
    the pangs of Sheol laid hold on me;
    I suffered distress and anguish.
Then I called on the name of the Lord,
    "O Lord, I pray, save my life!"

Gracious is the Lord and righteous;
    our God is merciful.
The Lord protects the simple;
    when I was brought low, he saved me.
Return, O my soul, to your rest,
    for the Lord has dealt bountifully with you.

For you have delivered my soul from death,
    my eyes from tears,
    my feet from stumbling.
I walk before the Lord
    in the land of the living.
I kept my faith, even when I said,
    "I am greatly afflicted";
I said in my consternation,
    "Everyone is a liar."

What shall I return to the Lord
  for all his bounty to me?
I will lift up the cup of salvation
  and call on the name of the Lord;
I will pay my vows to the Lord
  in the presence of all his people.
Precious in the sight of the Lord
  is the death of his faithful ones.
O Lord, I am your servant;
  I am your servant, the child of your serving girl.
  You have loosed my bonds.
I will offer to you a thanksgiving sacrifice
  and call on the name of the Lord.
I will pay my vows to the Lord
  in the presence of all his people,
in the courts of the house of the Lord,
  in your midst, O Jerusalem.
Praise the Lord!

The Ten Commandments

The Father: As we have sung and reflected on God's mighty deeds in delivering Israel from Egypt through the Psalms, let us now turn our thoughts to the journey of the Israelites through the wilderness.

At the Sea of Reeds, Moses led Israel through the waters, and they crossed the desert, eventually settling in the oasis of Kadesh-Barnea. There, they lived in tents and reed huts, much like Bedouins.

At the beginning of their journey through the desert, they arrived at a wilderness called Sinai and set up camp. It was there, on Mount Sinai, that Moses went up the mountain alone and received the commandments of God.

Let us now recall the Ten Commandments, which were given to guide us in living lives of holiness and righteousness.

All participants stand with heads covered.

All:

1. I am the Lord your God, who brought you out of the land of Egypt, out of the house of slavery. You shall have no other gods before me.
2. You shall not make for yourself an idol—no graven images or likenesses—nor bow down to them or serve them.
3. You shall not take the name of the Lord your God in vain.
4. Remember the Sabbath day, and keep it holy.
5. Honor your father and your mother.
6. You shall not kill.
7. You shall not commit adultery.
8. You shall not steal.
9. You shall not bear false witness against your neighbor.
10. You shall not covet.

Father: This is the Word of God as it is found in the Torah. Let us now drink the second cup of wine.

All: Blessed are You, O Lord our God, King of the Universe, Creator of the fruit of the vine.

All participants drink the second cup of wine, the Cup of Deliverance.

Washing with a Blessing

The Father: As we prepare to eat the matzah, we pause for the ritual washing of hands, known as Rachtzah. This washing reminds us that before we partake in the bread of life, we must come with clean hands and a pure heart. Let us wash our hands now, preparing to eat the matzah, the Bread of Life that God has given us.

All: Blessed are You, Lord our God, King of the universe, who has sanctified us with His commandments and commanded us concerning the washing of hands.

All participants wash their hands, reflecting quietly on their readiness to partake in the sacred meal. After washing, they dry their hands and prepare to continue with the next part of the Seder.

The Blessing and Breaking of the Bread

The Father: We now come to the part of the Seder where we eat the matzah, the unleavened bread that symbolizes both the haste of the Israelites' departure from Egypt and the bread of affliction that they ate. The Matzah reminds us of the struggles our ancestors faced and calls us to embrace humility and simplicity in our own lives. As we eat this bread, let us reflect on the spiritual nourishment that God provides us each day.

The Father breaks a matzah into small pieces and distributes them to everyone around the table. All participants remain standing with heads covered for the blessing over the bread.

All: Blessed are You, O Lord our God, King of the Universe, who brings forth bread from the earth. Blessed are You, O Lord our God, King of the Universe, who has sanctified us with His commandments and commanded us to eat unleavened bread.

Everyone eats a piece of the matzah they have received, and the remaining piece is kept for later. Participants then sit down.

The Bitter Herbs

The Father: Next, we partake in the bitter herbs, known as maror. These herbs symbolize the bitterness of slavery that our ancestors endured in Egypt. As we eat the maror, we remember the suffering and hardship that are part of the human condition, and we also remember that God, in His mercy, delivers us from our afflictions.

All: Blessed are You, Lord our God, King of the universe, who has sanctified us with His commandments and ordered us to eat bitter herbs.

In silence all participants eat a small amount of the bitter herbs.

The Hillel Sandwich

The Father: We now reach the tradition of Korech, or the Hillel Sandwich, introduced by Hillel the Elder, a revered Jewish sage. He combined matzah and maror—unleavened bread and bitter herbs—into a sandwich, symbolizing the blend of the bitterness of slavery with the sustenance and hope found in God's promises.

As we prepare to eat this sandwich, let us reflect on the moments in our lives when we have experienced both bitterness and hope. Just as matzah and maror are combined in this sandwich, so too are our experiences of suffering and redemption woven together in God's plan for our lives. May this act remind us that even in the midst of life's trials, God's promises sustain us, and His presence gives us hope.

The Father now takes the matzah and maror, combines them to form the sandwich, and begins eating, followed by all the participants. Everyone eats the sandwich in silence, reflecting on the blending of bitterness and hope.

The Festive Meal

The Father: With the matzah and bitter herbs eaten, we now come to the Shulchan Oreich, the festive meal. This is a time of joy and fellowship as we share in the abundance of God's provision. The meal reminds us of the richness of life that God grants us, even in times of struggle. As we eat together, let us reflect on the journey from slavery to freedom that we have remembered tonight. Let us enjoy this time, mindful of the blessings that God continually bestows upon us.

We also eat the lamb that the Lord our God has commanded us to eat. Let us remember the lamb that our ancestors slaughtered and ate roasted, without breaking any of its bones, just as the Lord commanded Moses. Let us recall the blood of the lamb that our ancestors spread on the doorposts and lintels of their homes, sparing their firstborn from death. This is the lamb by which we were delivered from the greatest of curses—the death of our firstborn.

All: Blessed are You, O Lord our God, King of the Universe, for saving our firstborn from death when Your destroying angel saw the sign of the lamb's blood—the sign of the covenant between You and us—and passed over without extending his mighty hand against our firstborn. Thus, You delivered us from the curse of death. You, our God, were merciful to us, and You freed us from bondage without bringing us into another. Blessed are You, O Lord our God, who has commanded us to eat the lamb, by whose blood we mark the doorposts of our homes.

The Father: Eat the lamb and the rest of the meal now. Consume everything that has been prepared, leaving only a spoonful of charoset, a little bit of the bitter herb sauce, and a small portion of the matzah to be reserved for later.

As we partake in this meal, let the atmosphere be filled with the joy of a family gathering. Traditionally, the women present, especially the mother, serve the table. After everyone has eaten, all plates with leftovers should be removed to continue the ritual, but the main plate remains. This transition marks a shift back to prayer, now offering thanks to God for all He has done for us.

During this time, participants may drink more wine if they wish, enjoying the freedom of celebration. This should be done in moderation, keeping in mind the spiritual significance of the meal. The third cup, which will be blessed later, should be reserved for its specific part in the ritual.

Christ's Words at the Last Supper

After the table has been cleared, you may wish to play some calm background music to create a peaceful atmosphere. If the lights were switched on during the meal, now they should be dimmed again, allowing the candles to dominate the room with their soft glow. Once everyone is settled, continue with the following part of the gathering, letting the gentle lighting and music guide participants into a reflective and serene state of mind.

The Father: Now that we have eaten, we pause to reflect on a moment that probably occurred at this point in the meal, when Jesus spoke intimately with His disciples during the Last Supper. As they gathered around the table, He shared words that would guide and comfort them, fully aware of what was to come. Tonight, we will recall some of those profound teachings, allowing them to speak to our hearts as they did to the disciples on that night.

Reader 1: "I am the vine, you are the branches. Those who abide in me and I in them bear much fruit, because apart from me you can do nothing." (John 15:5)

Reader 2: "As the Father has loved me, so I have loved you; abide in my love. If you keep my commandments, you will abide in my love, just as I have kept my Father's commandments and abide in His love." (John 15:9-10)

Reader 3: "I give you a new commandment, that you love one another. Just as I have loved you, you also should love one another. By this everyone will know that you are my disciples, if you have love for one another." (John 13:34-35)

Reader 4: "Those who love me will keep my word, and my Father will love them, and we will come to them and make our home with them. Whoever does not love me does not keep my words; and the word that you hear is not mine, but is from the Father who sent me." (John 14:23-24)

The Father: As we continue, we enter into the heart of Jesus' prayer for His disciples, known as the High Priestly Prayer. In these words, Jesus prays for His followers—both those with Him that night and all who would come after them, including us. He prays for our protection, our unity, and our sanctification. Let us listen to the highlights of this prayer, recognizing that Jesus' words are both a plea and a promise, meant to sustain us in our journey of faith.

Reader 5: "I glorified you on earth by finishing the work that you gave me to do. So now, Father, glorify me in your own presence with the glory that I had in your presence before the world existed. I have made your name known to those whom you gave me from the world. They were yours, and you gave them to me, and they have kept your word." (John 17:4-6)

Reader 6: "But now I am coming to you, and I speak these things in the world so that they may have my joy made complete in themselves. I have given them your word, and the world has hated them because they do not belong to the world, just as I do not belong to the world. I am not asking you to take them out of the world, but I ask you to protect them from the evil one. They do not belong to the world, just as I do not belong to the world. Sanctify them in the truth; your word is truth. As you have sent me into the world, so I have sent them into the world. And for their sakes I sanctify myself, so that they also may be sanctified in truth." (John 17:13-19)

The Father: These words from Jesus are more than just teachings; they are His prayer for us, spoken with love and concern for our well-being. Let us now proceed with the Seder, mindful of the deep connection we share with Christ and with one another through His love and sacrifice.

Eating the Afikoman

The Father: We now turn our attention to the Afikoman, the piece of matzah that was set aside and hidden earlier in the Seder. The Afikoman, representing the Paschal lamb that was eaten at the end of the meal during the first Passover, serves as the final food we eat tonight. Just as the Israelites sought redemption, we too search for the Afikoman, bringing it back to the table as a symbol of our ongoing journey toward wholeness and redemption in God's presence.

Let us now find the Afikoman, which was hidden earlier, and share it together as a sign of our unity and our hope in the promises of God.

The Afikoman is retrieved, and the father then gives each participant a piece of the Afikoman. After everyone has received their portion, the father proceeds with the blessing.

The Father: Blessed are You, Lord our God, King of the universe, who has sanctified us with Your commandments and commanded us to eat unleavened bread.

The Father: At this point in the meal, the Jews traditionally ate this piece of bread, which represented the Paschal lamb. However, on the night of the Last Supper, Jesus, who is the Lamb of God, took this same symbol of redemption and gave it a new and profound meaning. By taking the bread, He instituted the Eucharist, declaring, "This is my body, which is given for you; do this in remembrance of me."

The blessing we have just recited echoes the moment when Jesus gave thanks and shared this bread with His disciples, forever changing its significance. Let us now listen to the Gospel account of this sacred event.

A reading from the Holy Gospel according to Mark.

"While they were eating, he took a loaf of bread, and <u>after blessing it</u> he broke it, gave it to them, and said, 'Take; this is my body'" (Mark 14:22-24).

The Father: As Christ offered His body for our salvation, I, representing Christ in this rite, do not partake in this bread, for it symbolizes His own body, which He offered for us all. Instead, we partake in this bread as a symbol of the unity we share in His sacrifice. It is important to note that the bread we are eating now is not the Eucharist. We are simply re-enacting the moment when Christ instituted the Eucharist to better understand its profound meaning.

The participants eat the bread in silence.

The Cup of Redemption

The Father: In the Seder meal, after eating the Afikoman, which represents the Paschal lamb that saved the Israelites from Egypt, the third cup, known as the Cup of Redemption, is lifted, blessed, and drunk. This cup symbolizes the promise of God's deliverance, particularly the moment when their sons were spared from the final plague by the blood of the lamb on their doorposts. As Scripture says, "When I see the blood, I will pass over you, and no plague will befall you to destroy you when I strike the land of Egypt" (Exodus 12:13).

Through the events of Christ's passion, this redemption was fully realized in a new and profound way through His sacrifice on the cross. At the Last Supper, Jesus took this very cup and said, "This is my blood of the covenant, which is poured out for many." With these words, He instituted the Eucharist, establishing a new covenant sealed in His blood.

Let us now lift our cups and give thanks for the redemption that God has provided for us, both in the past and through the sacrifice of Christ.

All Participants lift their cups.

All Participants: Blessed are You, Lord our God, King of the universe, who creates the fruit of the vine.

The Father: Just as we earlier noted that the Jews ate the bread representing the Paschal lamb immediately after blessing it, they also drank the Cup of Redemption at this point in the meal, symbolizing their deliverance by the blood of the lamb. However, on the night of the Last Supper, Jesus, whose own blood would redeem us, took this same symbol and gave it a new and profound meaning. By taking the wine, He instituted the Eucharist, declaring, "This is my blood of the covenant, which is poured out for many." The blessing we have just recited reflects the exact moment when Jesus gave the cup, signifying His blood, to His disciples. Let us now listen to the Gospel account of this sacred event.

"Then he took a cup, and after giving thanks he gave it to them, and all of them drank from it. He said to them, 'This is my blood of the covenant, which is poured out for many. Truly I tell you, I will never again drink of the fruit of the vine until that day when I drink it new in the kingdom of God'" (Mark 14:24-25).

The Father: Now, you may drink the Cup of Redemption.

Everyone drinks the third cup of wine, except the father, who represents Christ.

Reflecting on the Institution of the Eucharist

The Father: Having eaten the bread and drunk the wine, let us now enter into a moment of deep reflective silence to contemplate the profound mystery we have just participated in. This moment is not merely a reenactment, but a spiritual connection to the very heart of our faith—the institution of the Eucharist.

On that sacred night, as Jesus gathered with His disciples, He summarized the entire story of salvation, a story that had been unfolding since the beginning of time. In this act, Jesus took the symbols of the Passover meal, the bread and the cup, and transformed them into the very essence of our salvation. The Eucharist is the pinnacle of this story, where the promise of redemption is fully realized through Christ's sacrifice.

In each Eucharistic prayer, especially in Eucharistic Prayer IV, we recount the narrative of salvation, from creation, through the covenant with Israel, to the sending of the Son, and finally, to the sacrifice on the cross and the resurrection. This prayer encapsulates the entire history of God's saving actions, culminating in the Eucharist, where we partake in the body and blood of Christ, the ultimate gift of love.

Let us now listen to the full Gospel account of the institution of the Eucharist, allowing these sacred words to speak deeply to our hearts, just as they did to the disciples on that night.

Gospel Reader: A reading from the Holy Gospel according to Mark (14:17-25).

> *"When it was evening, he came with the twelve. And when they had taken their places and were eating [...]. And while they were eating, he took a loaf of bread, and after blessing it he broke it, gave it to them, and said, 'Take; this is my body.' Then he took a cup, and after giving thanks he gave it to them, and all of them drank from it. He said to them, 'This is my blood of the covenant, which is poured out for many. Truly I tell you, I will never again drink of the fruit of the vine until that day when I drink it new in the kingdom of God.'"*

The Gospel of the Lord.

All: Praise to you, Lord Jesus Christ.

Elijah's Cup

The Father: As we come to this point in our Seder, we turn our attention to the cup traditionally left for Elijah the Prophet. In Jewish tradition, Elijah is expected to return as the forerunner of the Messiah, heralding the coming of the Kingdom of God. For us this cup holds a deeper significance.

Elijah symbolizes the prophetic hope of Israel—the anticipation of the coming Messiah, who would bring final redemption and establish God's Kingdom on earth. We believe that Jesus Christ is the fulfillment of this hope, the promised Messiah who has already come and brought redemption through His life, death, and resurrection. Yet, we also live in the "already but not yet" reality of God's Kingdom—where Christ has begun His reign, but we still await its completion.

Let us now fill a cup and set it aside for Elijah. As we do so, we remember the prophetic role of Elijah, who pointed toward the coming of the Messiah. We also look forward to Christ's return, when He will bring the fullness of God's Kingdom, making all things new.

The Father pours wine into a special cup and places it in the center of the table.

All Participants: Blessed are You, Lord our God, King of the universe, who has sent Your Son, Jesus Christ, as the fulfillment of Your promises. We remember the words of Your prophet Malachi: "Behold, I will send you the prophet Elijah before the great and terrible day of the Lord comes" (Malachi 4:5). May this cup remind us of the hope we have in Your unfailing promises and the coming of Your Kingdom.

The Father: As we set aside this cup for Elijah, let us reflect on the words of Jesus concerning the fulfillment of prophecy: "Truly I tell you, Elijah has already come, and they did not recognize him, but did to him whatever they pleased. So also the Son of Man is about to suffer at their hands." Then the disciples understood that he was speaking to them about John the Baptist (Matthew 17:12-13).

In this passage, Jesus identifies John the Baptist as the "Elijah" who was to come, preparing the way for the Messiah. Yet, just as the people did not recognize Elijah, so too was the Messiah misunderstood and rejected. As we consider this cup, let us renew our commitment to recognize Christ in our midst and to live in the hope of His return, when He will bring final redemption and peace to all creation.

All: Blessed are You, Lord our God, who sent John the Baptist to prepare the way for Your Son, Jesus Christ. May we be ready to welcome Christ when He comes again in glory.

Blessing of the Bitter Herbs

The Father: We now move to the second ritual dipping, where we fulfill the commandment to eat bitter herbs tonight. Earlier, we combined the bitterness and sweetness in the Korech, symbolizing the intertwining of suffering and hope. Now, we take a moment to focus specifically on the bitterness, acknowledging the suffering endured by our ancestors in Egypt.

This act also invites us to reflect on the profound meaning it held for Christ. As He participated in this very ritual during the Last Supper, He knew that His own Passion was imminent—the ultimate embodiment of suffering and sacrifice. Yet, just as the bitterness of the herbs is tempered by the sweetness of the charoset, so too was Christ's suffering followed by the triumph of His Resurrection. In this combination, we see the fullness of our salvation: the bitterness of the Cross and the sweetness of the Resurrection.

Now that we have eaten the Passover lamb, each of us will take a bit of the bitter herb sauce and dip it into the charoset, fulfilling the commandment to eat bitter herbs tonight. This is the second time we dip our food this evening, and it serves as a powerful reminder of the dual realities of suffering and redemption.

The Father: Take a small spoonful of the bitter herb sauce and, with the same spoon, take a bit of the charoset. This combination reminds us not only of the bitterness of slavery and the sweetness of freedom but also of the suffering Christ endured and the joy of His Resurrection.

Everyone: Blessed are You, Lord our God, King of the universe, who has sanctified us with His commandments and commanded us to eat bitter herbs.

The Father: Now, let us eat the remaining matzah with the bitter herbs, continuing this meal that reminds us of both the suffering and joy, the bondage and the freedom of our ancestors—and our own. As we do, let us also remember that through Christ, the bitterness of suffering is transformed into the sweetness of salvation.

The participants eat the remaining matzah along with the bitter herbs.

A Song of Gratitude: The Dayenu

The Father: As we reflect on the blessings we've experienced, both the sweetness of freedom and the bitterness of suffering, we now move into a moment of joyful gratitude with the singing of the Dayenu. This traditional song expresses our thanks for each of the many acts of grace that God has bestowed upon His people. The word "Dayenu" means **"It would have been enough for us!"**—a powerful acknowledgment that even if God had stopped at just one blessing, it would have been sufficient. Yet, His grace is abundant and beyond measure.

In singing the Dayenu, we celebrate each gift from God, recognizing that His generosity is far greater than we deserve. Traditionally, different members of the family recite or sing the verses, with everyone joining in the joyful refrain of "Da, Da, Dayenu!"

Before we begin, let us take a moment to rehearse the refrain together so that our hearts and voices are united in this expression of gratitude.

The Father: Has the One who is from everlasting to everlasting performed wonders for us?

Reader 1: If He had brought us out of Egypt but had not judged our enemies...

All: Da, Da, Dayenu!

Reader 2: If He had parted the sea for us but had not drowned those who pursued us…

All: Da, Da, Dayenu!

Reader 3: If He had saved us from those who pursued us but had not fed us manna in the desert…

All: Da, Da, Dayenu!

Reader 4: If He had fed us manna in the desert but had not given us the Sabbath…

All: Da, Da, Dayenu!

Reader 5: If He had given us the Sabbath but had not given us the Torah…

All: Da, Da, Dayenu!

Reader 6: If He had given us the Torah but had not brought us into the land of Israel…

All: Da, Da, Dayenu!

Reader 7: If He had brought us into the land of Israel but had not built His Temple…

All: Da, Da, Dayenu!

Recognizing the Fullness of God's Grace

The Father: The Dayenu not only allows us to reflect on the historical acts of God's grace but also invites us to recognize His ongoing blessings. As we continue, let us extend this song of gratitude to encompass the fullness of God's work in our salvation history:

Reader 8: If He had given us the Temple but had not sent us the prophets…

All: Da, Da, Dayenu!

Reader 9: If He had sent us the prophets but had not given us His only Son…

All: Da, Da, Dayenu!

Reader 10: If He had given us His only Son but had not allowed Him to teach and heal…

All: Da, Da, Dayenu!

Reader 11: If He had allowed Him to teach and heal but had not sacrificed Him on the cross for our sins…

All: Da, Da, Dayenu!

Reader 12: If He had sacrificed Him on the cross but had not raised Him from the dead…

All: Da, Da, Dayenu!

Reader 13: If He had raised Him from the dead but had not given us the Holy Spirit...

All: Da, Da, Dayenu!

A Prayer of Praise

The Father: As we conclude this powerful reflection on God's abundant grace, let us unite our hearts in a prayer of praise. Together, we will recite the Magnificat, the song of Mary, which captures the spirit of joyful gratitude that we have expressed in the Dayenu.

All:
"My soul magnifies the Lord,
and my spirit rejoices in God my Savior,
for he has looked with favor
on the lowliness of his servant.
Surely, from now on all generations
will call me blessed;
for the Mighty One
has done great things for me,
and holy is his name.
His mercy is for those who fear him
from generation to generation.
He has shown strength with his arm;
he has scattered the proud
in the thoughts of their hearts.
He has brought down the powerful

from their thrones,
and lifted up the lowly;
he has filled the hungry with good things,
and sent the rich away empty.
He has helped his servant Israel,
in remembrance of his mercy,
according to the promise
he made to our ancestors,
to Abraham and to his descendants forever."
(Luke 1:46-55).

The Father: We will now continue to praise the Lord with the recitation of Psalms 117 and 118, joining in the ancient song of God's people, who have always recognized His enduring mercy and love.

Psalm 117

Universal Call to Worship

Praise the Lord, all you nations!
   Extol him, all you peoples!
For great is his steadfast love toward us,
   and the faithfulness of the Lord endures forever.
Praise the Lord!

Psalm 118

A Song of Victory

O give thanks to the Lord, for he is good;
  his steadfast love endures forever!

Let Israel say,
  "His steadfast love endures forever."
Let the house of Aaron say,
  "His steadfast love endures forever."
Let those who fear the Lord say,
  "His steadfast love endures forever."

Out of my distress I called on the Lord;
  the Lord answered me and set me in a broad place.
With the Lord on my side I do not fear.
  What can mortals do to me?
The Lord is on my side to help me;
  I shall look in triumph on those who hate me.
It is better to take refuge in the Lord
  than to put confidence in mortals.
It is better to take refuge in the Lord
  than to put confidence in princes.

All nations surrounded me;
  in the name of the Lord I cut them off!
They surrounded me, surrounded me on every side;
  in the name of the Lord I cut them off!
They surrounded me like bees;
  they blazed like a fire of thorns;

in the name of the Lord I cut them off!
I was pushed hard, so that I was falling,
   but the Lord helped me.
The Lord is my strength and my might;
   he has become my salvation.

"The right hand of the Lord does valiantly;
   the right hand of the Lord is exalted;
   the right hand of the Lord does valiantly."
I shall not die, but I shall live
   and recount the deeds of the Lord.
The Lord has punished me severely,
   but he did not give me over to death.

Open to me the gates of righteousness,
   that I may enter through them
   and give thanks to the Lord.

This is the gate of the Lord;
   the righteous shall enter through it.

I thank you that you have answered me
   and have become my salvation.
The stone that the builders rejected
   has become the chief cornerstone.
This is the Lord's doing;
   it is marvelous in our eyes.
This is the day that the Lord has made;
   let us rejoice and be glad in it.
Save us, we beseech you, O Lord!
   O Lord, we beseech you, give us success!

Blessed is the one who comes in the name of
the Lord.[
    We bless you from the house of the Lord.
The Lord is God,
    and he has given us light.
Bind the festal procession with branches,
    up to the horns of the altar.

You are my God, and I will give thanks to you;
    you are my God; I will extol you.

O give thanks to the Lord, for he is good,
    for his steadfast love endures forever.

The Cup of Freedom

The Father: As we reach the conclusion of our Seder, we come to a moment filled with reflection and anticipation. This is Nirtzah, the closing of our Seder. The word "Nirtzah" means "accepted," signifying our hope that the prayers and rituals we have performed tonight are pleasing to God and accepted by Him.

Throughout this Seder, we have journeyed through the story of our ancestors' deliverance, shared in the symbols of their faith, and connected these ancient traditions to the fulfillment found in Christ. We have been reminded of God's faithfulness, not only in the past but also in the present and the future. As we conclude, we look forward with hope, confident in God's promises and the ongoing redemption He offers.

Now, we raise the fourth and final cup of wine, known as the CUP OF FREEDOM. This cup represents the fullness of God's redemption, not just for the Israelites in Egypt, but for all of humanity through Christ. It symbolizes the ultimate freedom that awaits us in God's kingdom, a freedom that was secured through the sacrifice of our Savior.

Let us now lift our cups and give thanks for the redemption that God has provided for us, both in the past and through the sacrifice of Christ.

All Participants: Blessed are You, Lord our God, King of the universe, who creates the fruit of the vine.

The Father: Let us drink the fourth cup, the Cup of Freedom, in gratitude for all that God has done and will do for us.

All participants drink the fourth cup of wine, the Cup of Freedom, but do not drink it all at this point, leaving some in the cup for the final blessing and declaration.

Looking Forward: Next Year in Jerusalem

The Father: Our Seder does not end here. With this final cup, we also look forward to the future—both the immediate future, with the hope of celebrating next year in Jerusalem, and the ultimate future, when we will celebrate in the Kingdom of God with Christ. The Seder is a reminder that our story is part of God's larger story, and that we are journeying towards a time when all things will be made new.

Let us lift our cups together and say, "Next year in Jerusalem!" as a sign of our hope in God's continued faithfulness and the fulfillment of His promises.

All: Next year in Jerusalem!

Everyone now drinks what is left of the fourth cup.

The Father: Before we part ways, let us end our Seder with a song that has been sung by our ancestors for generations. As we sing, let us carry the spirit of this meal into our daily lives, living out the freedom and redemption we have celebrated tonight.

Closing Songs

As we draw our Seder to a close, the journey we've undertaken tonight through the rich history of God's deliverance is sealed with songs of praise and hope. These closing songs are more than just tradition—they are a powerful way to encapsulate the themes of the evening: God's faithfulness, our gratitude, and the enduring promise of redemption.

The songs you choose to conclude your Seder can connect you deeply with the experiences of your ancestors while also allowing you to express your own faith and hope. Below are a few options, each carrying its own significance and tradition. Feel free to choose the ones that resonate most with you and your family or community.

1. Chad Gadya (One Little Goat)

"Chad Gadya" is a traditional song that may seem playful at first but carries deep spiritual meaning. Sung in Aramaic, it tells a repetitive story of a little goat bought by a father for two coins. Each verse adds new characters or events, ultimately leading to a divine intervention that brings justice and restoration.

This song symbolizes the Jewish people's history of oppression and deliverance, with the little goat representing the innocent and vulnerable, and God stepping in at the end to bring justice. As you sing "Chad Gadya," reflect on the cyclical nature of history and the constant presence of God's justice, love, and protection.

English Translation:

One little goat, one little goat,
My father bought for two zuzim,
one little goat, one little goat.
Then came the cat and ate the goat,
My father bought for two zuzim,
one little goat, one little goat.
...(the song continues, adding more elements with each verse)
Then came the Holy One, blessed be He,
And destroyed the Angel of Death,
Who killed the butcher,
Who slaughtered the ox,
That drank the water,
That quenched the fire,
That burned the stick,
That beat the dog,
That bit the cat,
That ate the goat,
My father bought for two zuzim,
one little goat, one little goat.

Explanation of Meaning:

- **The Little Goat:** Represents the Jewish people or, more broadly, the innocent and vulnerable.

- **The Father:** Symbolizes God, who cares for and protects His people.

- **Two Coins:** Could represent the two tablets of the Ten Commandments, symbolizing the covenant between God and His people.

- **The Cat, Dog, Stick, Fire, Water, Ox, Butcher, Angel of Death:** Each represents various oppressors or forces throughout history, with God ultimately intervening to bring justice.

This song reminds us that no matter the challenges faced, God's justice and redemption will prevail.

2. Adir Hu (Mighty is He)

"Adir Hu" is a hymn that praises God and expresses hope for the rebuilding of the Temple in Jerusalem. It is a powerful reminder of God's might and the enduring hope for restoration and peace. This song is a fitting conclusion to the Seder, as it looks forward to a future filled with God's presence and the fulfillment of His promises.

English Translation: Mighty is He, Mighty is He, Mighty is our Lord, who will soon build His house. Speedily, speedily, speedily and in our days soon, God, build, God, build, God, build Your house speedily.

3. Alternative Songs

If you prefer, you can choose other hymns that resonate with your faith and the themes of the Seder. Singing "Hallelujah" or a hymn like "Great Is Thy Faithfulness" can also be a beautiful way to close the Seder. While these songs are not traditional to the Seder, they carry a universal message of praise and gratitude to God. They connect the ancient traditions to our modern expressions of faith, allowing you to end the evening with hearts lifted in worship.

With these songs, we conclude the Seder in a spirit of joy, gratitude, and hopeful anticipation. The songs you sing are more than just a ritual—they are an offering of thanks, a proclamation of faith, and a reminder that we are part of God's ongoing story of redemption.

End of Seder

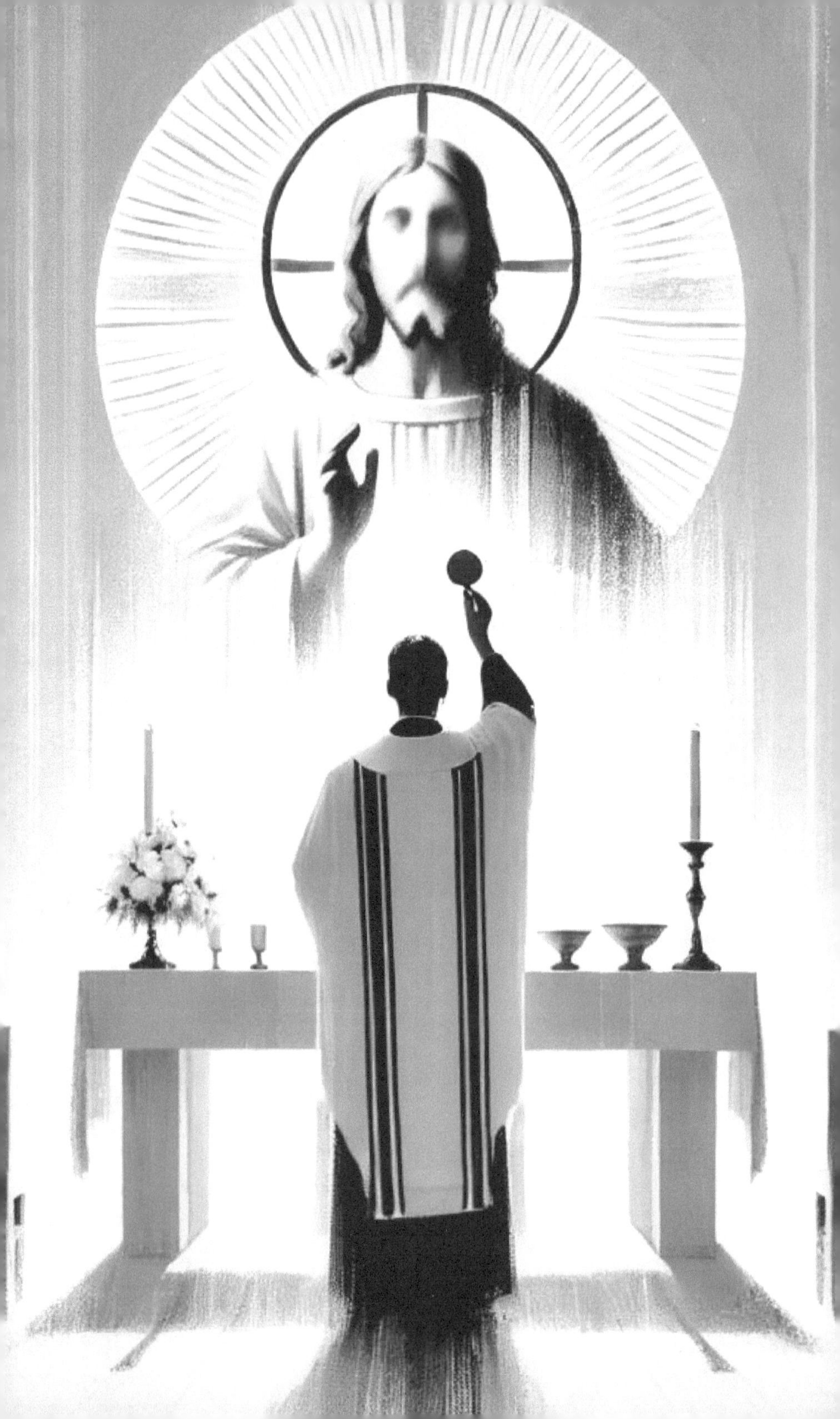

PART 5

THE EUCHARIST
AND
THE SEDER

Understanding the Eucharist Through the Seder

To be read by the participants individually or as a group after the Seder Celebration for further understanding of the connection between the Seder meal and the Eucharist.

A Journey of Faith and Fulfillment

As we conclude this profound journey through the Seder meal, we now stand at a unique crossroads where the richness of Jewish tradition meets the fulfillment of Christian faith. Having walked through each step of the Seder, you have experienced firsthand the deep symbolism that our ancestors in faith held dear. But more than that, you have now seen how these ancient practices were not only a remembrance of God's past deliverance but also a foreshadowing of the ultimate redemption brought by Christ.

This final chapter offers theological reflections that will help you further understand the profound connections between the Seder and the Eucharist. Each part of the Seder, which you have just participated in, points toward the sacrifice of Christ and the gift of the Eucharist—a sacrament that fulfills and transcends the Passover meal. Through these reflections, we will explore how the breaking of bread, the sharing of wine, and the retelling of salvation history are not only rooted in Jewish tradition but are also deeply embedded in our Christian faith.

As you read these reflections, consider how the Seder has enriched your understanding of the Eucharist. The meal you have just shared is more than a ritual; it is a doorway into the mysteries of our faith, revealing how God's plan for salvation has been unfolding throughout history. The Eucharist, which we celebrate as the source and summit of our Christian life, is illuminated through the lens of the Seder, allowing us to appreciate more fully the depth of Christ's sacrifice and the hope of eternal life with Him.

May these reflections deepen your love for the Eucharist and inspire you to approach it with a renewed sense of awe and gratitude, knowing that it is both the fulfillment of God's promises and a continual invitation to partake in the divine life offered to us through Christ.

The Role of the Covenant: A Foundation of Faith

At the heart of both the Seder and the Eucharist is the concept of the covenant—a sacred agreement between God and His people. The Seder commemorates the covenant God made with Israel, delivered through Moses, when He brought the Israelites out of Egypt. This covenant was sealed by the blood of the Passover lamb, a symbol of protection and deliverance.

In Christian theology, the Eucharist is understood as the celebration of the new and eternal covenant, instituted by Christ at the Last Supper. Just as the blood of the Passover lamb protected the Israelites, the blood of Christ, the Lamb of God, seals the new covenant, offering redemption and eternal life to all who believe. The Eucharist, therefore, is not just a ritual meal but a participation in this new covenant, reminding us of God's faithfulness and calling us to live out our covenantal relationship with Him.

Anamnesis: The Power of Sacred Memory

Both the Seder and the Eucharist are acts of sacred remembrance, known in Christian theology as anamnesis. In the Seder, the Jewish people recall God's mighty deeds in the Exodus, making those events present in their lives through ritual. The retelling of the Exodus story is not just a remembrance of the past but a way to experience God's deliverance in the present.

Similarly, in the Eucharist, Christians remember and make present the sacrifice of Christ. The words "Do this in remembrance of me," spoken by Jesus at the Last Supper, call us to enter into the Paschal

Mystery—Christ's passion, death, and resurrection—as a living reality. This act of remembrance is a powerful way in which both Jewish and Christian communities experience the ongoing faithfulness of God, ensuring that the saving acts of God are never confined to the past but continue to impact the present.

The Lighting of the Candles: Christ, the Light of the World

In the Seder, the lighting of the candles marks the beginning of the sacred meal. From a Christian perspective, this act symbolizes the light of Christ entering the world, illuminating our lives and guiding us on our spiritual journey. Just as the candles light up the physical space, Christ, the Light of the World, illuminates our hearts, bringing clarity, warmth, and hope to our faith. This light, which began with the incarnation of Christ, continues to guide us toward the fullness of life in Him, making each Eucharistic celebration a moment of spiritual enlightenment and grace.

The First Cup (Cup of Sanctification): A Call to Holiness

The first cup in the Seder, known as the Cup of Sanctification, reflects God's promise to "bring out" the Israelites from their burdens (Exodus 6:6). For Christians, this cup represents our sanctification through Christ, who frees us from the bondage of sin.

In the Eucharist, we are reminded of this ongoing sanctification and our call to holiness, as Christ sets us apart for God's purpose. This cup invites us to reflect on the transformative power of grace in our lives, urging us to live in a way that is pleasing to God, sanctified by the sacrificial love of Christ.

The Breaking of the Matzah (Afikoman): Christ's Sacrifice and Resurrection

During the Seder, the matzah is broken, and part of it, the Afikoman, is hidden away to be found later. In Christian theology, this action prefigures Christ's sacrifice. The broken matzah represents His broken body on the cross, hidden away in death, and later revealed in the resurrection. Just as the Afikoman is searched for and found, Christ's resurrection is the ultimate revelation of God's victory over sin and death. The Eucharist, in turn, becomes the sacred moment when we encounter the risen Christ, who offers Himself to us as the Bread of Life, nourishing our souls with His divine presence.

The Significance of the Unleavened Bread: Purity and Sacrifice

In the Seder, the unleavened bread (matzah) symbolizes the haste with which the Israelites left Egypt, not having time to let their bread rise. It also represents purity, being free from leaven, which is often seen as a symbol of sin.

For Christians, the breaking of the matzah during the Seder prefigures the breaking of Christ's body on the cross. The matzah, with its stripes and piercings, is a powerful symbol of Christ, who is described in Scripture as "wounded for our transgressions" (Isaiah 53:5). When we partake in the Eucharist, we receive the "Bread of Life," Christ's body, which was broken for our salvation. The matzah's simplicity and purity remind us of Christ's sinless life and His willing sacrifice for humanity.

The Second Cup (Cup of Deliverance): The New Covenant in Christ's Blood

The Cup of Deliverance in the Seder recalls God's promise to "rescue" the Israelites from slavery. In Christian thought, this cup symbolizes our deliverance from the power of sin and death through Christ's sacrifice. As we partake in the Eucharist, we drink of the new covenant, remembering how Christ's blood was shed for our salvation, delivering us from eternal separation from God. This cup, therefore, becomes a sign of the new covenant, inviting us to live in the freedom of Christ's redeeming love and to share in the mission of bringing this deliverance to the world.

The Eating of Bitter Herbs (Maror): Reflecting on Suffering and Redemption

The bitter herbs in the Seder remind participants of the bitterness of slavery in Egypt. For Christians, these herbs symbolize the bitterness of sin and the suffering Christ endured on our behalf. The Eucharist, while a celebration, also calls us to remember the suffering of Christ, who bore the weight of our sins and the bitterness of the cross to bring us freedom and new life. In this ritual, we are reminded of the cost of our redemption and the depth of Christ's love, which transforms suffering into a pathway to eternal life.

The Third Cup (Cup of Redemption): The Blood of Christ, Our Redemption

This cup represents God's promise to "redeem" the Israelites with an outstretched arm. In Christian belief, this cup is deeply connected to Christ's words at the Last Supper, where He identifies the cup with His blood, poured out for the redemption of many (Luke 22:20). Although Christ refrained from drinking this cup during the Last Supper, it points to the redemption achieved through His sacrifice on the cross, a redemption celebrated and made present in the Eucharist. As we drink from this cup, we are drawn into the mystery of Christ's passion and resurrection, participating in the redemption that He won for us through His sacrificial love.

The Cup of Elijah: Anticipation and Fulfillment

During the Seder, a cup is traditionally set aside for Elijah, the prophet who is expected to return before the coming of the Messiah. This cup symbolizes the hope and anticipation of the Messiah's arrival and the fulfillment of God's promises.

For Christians, this cup takes on a deeper significance. Jesus identifies John the Baptist as the "Elijah" who was to come (Matthew 17:12-13), preparing the way for Christ, the Messiah. The Eucharist, celebrated in the context of Christ's first coming, also points forward to His second coming, when He will return in glory to fully establish God's kingdom. The Cup of Elijah, therefore, can be seen as a symbol of both the anticipation of Christ's return and the fulfillment of God's redemptive plan.

The Fourth Cup (Cup of Praise): Anticipating the Heavenly Banquet

The final cup in the Seder is the Cup of Praise, celebrating God's promise to "take" the Israelites as His own people. For Christians, this cup reflects the joy and thanksgiving we express in the Eucharist, where we give praise for the new covenant established in Christ's blood. It also anticipates the fulfillment of God's kingdom, when Christ will drink this cup anew with us in the heavenly banquet (Matthew 26:29). This final cup, therefore, serves as a reminder of the eschatological hope that sustains us, pointing us toward the ultimate fulfillment of all God's promises in the joy of eternal life with Him.

The Singing of the Hallel Psalms: Praising God for Deliverance

The Hallel Psalms (113-118), sung during the Seder, are psalms of praise and thanksgiving for God's deliverance. In the Christian tradition, these psalms take on a deeper meaning as they are sung in light of Christ's ultimate deliverance of humanity through His death and resurrection. The Hallel reminds us of the ongoing need to praise God for His works and to look forward to the final redemption in Christ. As we sing these psalms in the context of the Eucharist, we join our voices with the chorus of saints and angels, offering praise to the God who saves us and brings us into the fullness of His kingdom.

The Passover Lamb: Christ, the True Lamb of God

The Passover lamb, central to the Seder, represents the sacrifice that spared the Israelites from the plague of the firstborn. In Christian theology, Christ is seen as the true Passover Lamb, whose sacrificial death spares us from eternal death. The Eucharist is the new Passover, where we partake in the Lamb of God, who takes away the sins of the world, offering us the promise of eternal life. In this sacred meal, we encounter Christ, the Lamb who was slain, and receive the grace that flows from His redemptive sacrifice, nourishing us and uniting us with Him in the hope of the resurrection.

The Role of Family and Community: Faith Lived Together

The Seder is traditionally a family-centered event, emphasizing the importance of passing on the faith from one generation to the next. It is a time for families to gather, retell the story of God's deliverance, and strengthen their bonds of faith and community.

Similarly, the Eucharist is not just a personal experience but a communal one. It is the sacrament that unites the Christian community as the Body of Christ. In the Eucharist, we are reminded that we are part of a larger faith community, called to support one another and live out our faith in unity. Reflecting on the communal aspects of both the Seder and the Eucharist highlights the importance of living our faith in community, where we are nourished and strengthened together.

The Concept of Sacrifice: Offering and Redemption

The Passover lamb, central to the Seder, represents the sacrifice that spared the Israelites from the plague of the firstborn. In Christian theology, Christ is the true Passover Lamb, whose sacrificial death on the cross spares us from eternal death. The Eucharist is the new Passover, where we partake in the Lamb of God, who takes away the sins of the world.

Sacrifice is a central theme in both the Seder and the Eucharist. In the Seder, the sacrifice of the lamb is a reminder of God's deliverance. In the Eucharist, Christ's sacrifice is the ultimate offering, through which we are redeemed. This connection between the two sacrifices deepens our understanding of the Eucharist as not only a memorial of Christ's death but also as a participation in the ongoing reality of His redemptive work.

Conclusion: A Journey from Tradition to Fulfillment

Each part of the Seder meal is rich in meaning and offers Christians a profound way to connect with the roots of their faith. By reflecting on these elements in light of Christ's life, death, and resurrection, we gain a deeper understanding of the Eucharist as the fulfillment of God's promises and a foretaste of the heavenly banquet to come.

The Seder and the Eucharist together tell the story of God's unceasing love and faithfulness—a story that began with the liberation of Israel from Egypt and reaches its fulfillment in the redemptive sacrifice of Christ. As you reflect on these connections, may your love for the Eucharist deepen, inspiring you to approach it with renewed awe and gratitude. In this sacred meal, we find the convergence of history, tradition, and divine grace, reminding us that we are part of God's ongoing story of salvation.

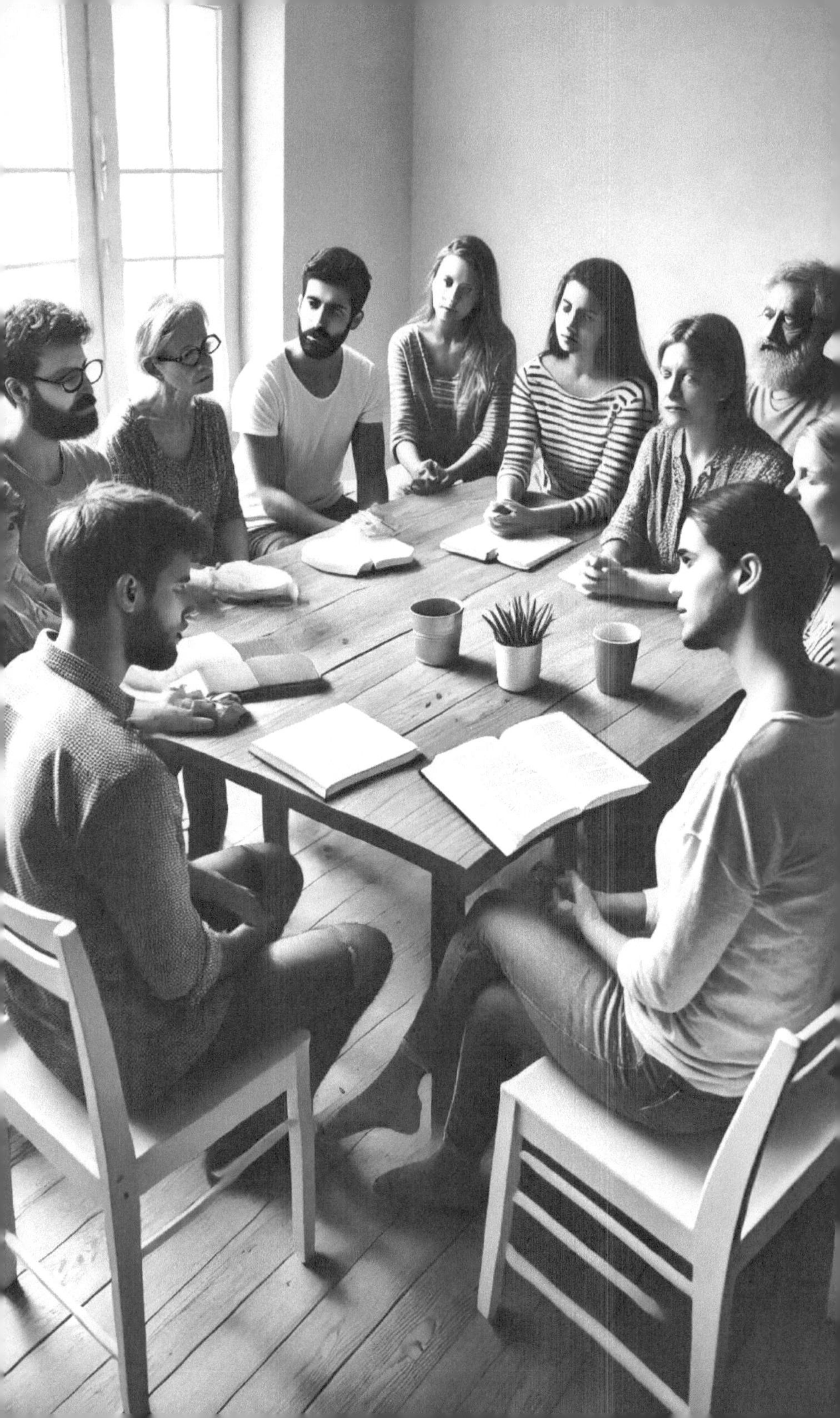

PART 6

GROUP STUDY GUIDE

Engaging with this **Group Study Guide** offers your group a unique opportunity to deepen your faith by exploring the rich connections between the Seder meal and the Eucharist. Whether you're a group of youths, couples, retirees, or simply a community seeking to grow together spiritually, this program provides a structured and meaningful way to understand and celebrate these sacred traditions.

Why should your group go through this program? Because it's more than just learning; it's about experiencing a profound journey of faith. Through these sessions, you'll uncover the historical and spiritual significance of the Seder and see how it beautifully connects to the heart of our Christian faith—the Eucharist. The reflections and discussions will not only deepen your understanding but also enrich your experience of these sacred practices, fostering a stronger sense of community and spiritual growth.

This guide includes four Lesson Plans:

- **Exploring the Seder Tradition:** Learn about the origins and significance of the Seder meal and its connection to the Eucharist.

- **Christ's Teachings During His Last Seder:** Reflect on the key teachings Jesus shared at the Last Supper and how they deepen our understanding of the Eucharist.

- **Getting Ready for the Seder:** Prepare both practically and spiritually for the Seder meal, ensuring a meaningful and sacred experience.

- **Understanding the Eucharist Through the Seder:** Reflect on the Seder experience and gain a deeper appreciation for the Eucharist as its fulfillment.

This study guide is suitable for use throughout the year but is especially well-suited for the liturgical seasons of **Lent and Eastertime**, as it aligns with the themes of preparation, sacrifice, and redemption.

By following this Group Study Guide, your group will be well-prepared to experience the Seder with a deeper understanding and to reflect on its significance in light of the Eucharist, enriching your faith journey as a community.

Lesson 1: Discovering the Roots

Exploring the Seder Tradition

Objective: To help the group understand the significance of the Seder meal and its connection to the Eucharist through a guided reading and discussion of the section "The Seder Tradition."

Lesson Plan

1. Opening Prayer (5 minutes)

Leader: Heavenly Father, we come together today to deepen our understanding of the sacred traditions that connect us to You. As we explore the Seder meal and its transformation into the Eucharist, open our hearts to the richness of these ancient practices. Help us to see Your guiding hand throughout history and feel Your presence with us today. May our discussions be filled with insight, and may our hearts be drawn closer to You. We ask this in the name of Jesus Christ, our Lord. Amen.

2. Introduction to the Lesson (5 minutes)

Leader: Today, we'll be diving into the first part of our guide, titled "The Seder Tradition." This section is divided into four main parts:

1. **The Sacred Meal**
2. **The Exodus: A Story of Freedom**
3. **From the Seder to the Last Supper**
4. **The Seder's Lasting Impact**

Each part provides key insights into the roots of the Seder meal and how it connects to the Eucharist. We'll break into small groups to read and discuss these sections, followed by a summary presentation.

Note: For a more efficient discussion, participants are encouraged to read their assigned sections at home before the meeting.

3. Group Reading (25 minutes)

Leader: At this point, the group will be divided into four smaller groups, with each group assigned one of the four sections. You will have 20 minutes to read through and discuss your assigned section together. Afterward, each group will choose one member to present the main insights to the entire group in no more than 2 minutes. To help with this, we've provided the main points of each chapter below.

Summary Points for Each Chapter

The Sacred Meal

- The Seder meal is a central tradition in the Jewish faith.
- It's filled with symbolism that tells the story of God's deliverance.
- The meal involves specific foods that represent elements of the Exodus story.
- It is more than just a meal; it's a living tradition passed down through generations.
- Understanding this meal helps us appreciate the depth of the Eucharist.

The Exodus: A Story of Freedom

- The Israelites were enslaved in Egypt, facing great suffering.
- God commanded a special meal, the first Passover, before their escape.
- The meal included lamb, unleavened bread, and bitter herbs, each with deep symbolism.
- This event, the Exodus, became a defining moment in Israel's history.
- The Passover meal evolved into the Seder, a lasting tradition of remembrance.

From the Seder to the Last Supper

- Jesus and His disciples observed the Seder during the Last Supper.

- Jesus gave new meaning to the Seder by transforming it into the Eucharist.
- The bread and wine were symbols of His body and blood, establishing a new covenant.
- This act connected the old tradition to the new Christian practice.
- The Eucharist is rooted in the Seder but represents a new promise for all humanity.

The Seder's Lasting Impact

- The Seder remains a living tradition that continues to shape faith.
- It connects participants with the story of God's deliverance.
- For Christians, it provides a deeper understanding of the Eucharist.
- The Seder shows how ancient practices are fulfilled in Christ.
- It serves as a reminder of God's ongoing story of salvation.

4. Group Discussion (20 minutes)

Discussion Questions:

- What did your group find most significant about the section you read?
- How does understanding the Seder meal change your perspective on the Eucharist?
- What new connections between the Old and New Testaments did you discover?

- How can these insights influence your personal faith journey?

Encourage each group to share their thoughts and engage in a meaningful discussion based on the summary points and questions.

5. Closing Prayer (5 minutes):

Leader: Gracious God, thank You for the time we've spent together in learning and reflection. As we leave this gathering, may the lessons of the Seder and the Eucharist continue to inspire us and deepen our relationship with You. Help us to carry the meaning of these sacred traditions into our lives, living out the love and sacrifice that Jesus showed us. We ask this in His holy name. Amen.

Lesson 2: Jesus' Final Teachings

Christ's Teachings During His Last Seder

Objective: To help the group understand and reflect on the profound teachings of Jesus during the Last Supper, and how these teachings connect to the Seder meal and the Eucharist.

Lesson Plan

1. Opening Prayer (5 minutes)

Leader: Heavenly Father, as we gather today, we ask for Your guidance and wisdom. Open our hearts to the teachings of Jesus during His Last Supper, so that we may understand the depth of His love and the significance of His final words. May these teachings shape our hearts and lives, leading us closer to You. We ask this in the name of Jesus Christ, our Lord. Amen.

2. Introduction to the Lesson (5 minutes)

Leader: Today, we'll be reflecting on the key teachings Jesus shared with His disciples during His Last Seder, as recorded in the Gospels. These teachings are central to our faith and provide deep insights into the meaning of the Eucharist and the Seder. We'll divide into smaller groups to explore each teaching in detail, followed by a summary presentation.

3. Group Reading (25 minutes)

Leader: Divide the group into four smaller groups, with each group assigned one of the following teachings to read and discuss. You will have 20 minutes to read through your assigned section together. Afterward, each group will choose one member to present the main insights to the entire group in no more than 2 minutes.

Summary Points for Each Chapter

The New Commandment: Love One Another

- Jesus introduced a new commandment focused on self-giving love.
- This love is the foundation of Christian life and community.
- It calls for sacrificial love, mirroring Christ's own love for us.

- This commandment is central to our identity as Christ's disciples.
- Reflecting on this teaching prepares us to love others as Christ loved us.

The Promise of the Holy Spirit

- Jesus promised the Holy Spirit as an Advocate and Guide.
- The Holy Spirit empowers and teaches us, continuing Jesus' work.
- This promise assures us of Christ's ongoing presence in our lives.
- The Holy Spirit transforms and strengthens us for service.
- Reflecting on this promise helps us rely on the Spirit's guidance and strength.

Abiding in Christ, the True Vine

- Jesus emphasized the importance of staying connected to Him.
- Abiding in Christ leads to spiritual growth and fruitfulness.
- Pruning by the Father helps us become more fruitful.
- This connection is vital for living a true Christian life.
- Reflecting on this teaching reminds us to stay rooted in Christ's love.

Christ's Prayer for His Disciples

- Jesus prayed for unity, protection, and sanctification for His disciples.
- This prayer extends to all believers, emphasizing our call to holiness.
- Jesus' prayer highlights the importance of living in unity and truth.
- The promise of eternal life is central to this prayer.
- Reflecting on this prayer encourages us to live out Christ's desires for His followers.

4. Group Discussion (20 minutes)

Discussion Questions:

- What did your group find most significant about the teaching you discussed?
- How do these teachings connect to the Seder and the Eucharist?
- What new insights have you gained about living out these teachings in your daily life?
- How can these teachings deepen our experience of the Seder meal?

Encourage each group to share their thoughts and engage in a meaningful discussion based on the summary points and questions.

5. Closing Prayer (5 minutes)

Leader: Gracious God, thank You for the time we've spent reflecting on the teachings of Jesus during His Last Supper. As we leave this gathering, may these teachings continue to resonate in our hearts, guiding us in our faith and drawing us closer to You. Help us to live out the love, unity, and faithfulness that Jesus exemplified. We ask this in His holy name. Amen.

Lesson 3: Preparing the Table

Getting Ready for the Seder

> **Objective:** To guide the group in the practical and spiritual preparations for the Seder meal, ensuring everyone understands the significance of each element and is ready to participate fully.

Lesson Plan

1. Opening Prayer (5 minutes)

Leader: Heavenly Father, as we gather to prepare for the Seder, we ask for Your guidance and blessing. Help us to understand the deep meaning behind each element of this sacred meal and to approach our preparations with hearts full of reverence and gratitude. May this time of preparation draw us closer to You and to one another. We ask this in the name of Jesus Christ, our Lord. Amen.

2. Introduction to the Lesson (5 minutes)

Leader: Today, we'll be focusing on the practical and spiritual preparations for the Seder meal. This includes everything from setting the table to understanding the symbolic foods and the roles each person will play during the meal. We'll also take a look at the recipes provided in the appendix to ensure we're familiar with the foods we'll be preparing and their significance.

3. Group Reading (25 minutes)

Leader: Divide the group into smaller teams to review the following sections:

The Ritual Preparations

- Focus on preparing the symbolic foods: matzah, karpas, maror, charoset, and wine.
- Understand the spiritual meaning behind each item and how they will be used during the Seder.

Setting the Table

- Discuss how to create a sacred and inviting space for the Seder.
- Ensure everyone knows how to arrange the symbolic foods, candles, and tableware to reflect the significance of the meal.

The Dynamics and Roles During the Seder Meal

- Review the roles of the father, mother, children, and other participants.
- Understand how these roles help bring the Seder to life and foster a sense of unity.

Creating the Spiritual Atmosphere

- Explore ways to cultivate a reflective and sacred environment.
- Consider the use of music, scripture readings, and prayers to enhance the spiritual experience.

Recipes Review and Initial Planning

Encourage each small team to spend a few minutes reviewing the recipes in the appendix.

Understanding how to prepare the Seder foods not only ensures the meal is authentic but also deepens your connection to the traditions and symbolism of the Seder.

As they review, each group can start considering what they are able to prepare and what resources they might need.

This initial discussion will help everyone gauge their capabilities and think about how they can contribute to the meal preparation.

4. Group Discussion and Cooking Organization (20+ minutes)

Discussion Questions:

- What stood out to you about the preparation of the symbolic foods?
- How can we create a table setting that feels sacred and inviting?
- How do the different roles during the Seder contribute to the overall experience?
- What elements can we include to enhance the spiritual atmosphere of the Seder?

As you discuss these questions, encourage each group to think practically about how they can contribute to the Seder meal. This is an opportunity for everyone to share ideas and ensure that all aspects of the meal are thoughtfully prepared.

Group Cooking Organization

After the discussion, smoothly transition into organizing the group for meal preparation. Begin assigning specific tasks and roles to different participants. Consider holding a group cooking session where everyone can come together to prepare the meal, fostering fellowship and ensuring that each dish is made with care. The cooking organization can be finalized during this encounter, or you may choose to schedule a separate meeting focused entirely on meal preparation.

Invite Others to Join the Seder

Consider inviting other family members, friends, or community members to join the Seder meal. Opening up the Seder to a broader group can enrich the experience by bringing together different perspectives and creating a deeper sense of community.

Complete Checklist for the Seder Meal

During this meeting, review the following tasks and assign responsibilities:

- **Cooking the Lamb**
- **Buying the Wine or Grape Juice**
- **Bringing Candles**
- **Preparing the Charoset**
- **Preparing the Matzah and Bitter Herbs**
- **Preparing the Eggs**
- **Decorating the Space:** Create a sacred and inviting atmosphere.
- **Assigning the Seder Roles:** Ensure everyone knows their part (Father/Presider, Mother, Youngest Child, Readers, Commentator).

- **Checking for Allergies:** Confirm that all foods are safe for everyone.
- **Organizing Transportation:** Plan for designated drivers or arrange alternative transportation, considering the consumption of four glasses of wine per person.

By the end of this session, ensure that all roles are clearly assigned and that each participant knows their responsibilities. This preparation will help your group come together to create a meaningful and spiritually enriching Seder experience, with the added joy and depth that comes from sharing it with a larger community.

5. Closing Prayer (5 minutes)

Leader: Gracious God, thank You for this time of preparation. As we draw closer to the Seder, help us to carry forward what we've learned today. May our efforts in preparing this meal be a reflection of our desire to honor You and to enter more deeply into the story of Your deliverance. Guide us as we move forward, and may our Seder be a time of profound spiritual renewal. We ask this in Jesus' name. Amen.

The next encounter will be the Seder meal.

Lesson 4: From Seder to Eucharist

Understanding the Eucharist Through the Seder

> **Objective:** To help participants reflect on their experience of the Seder meal and deepen their understanding of the Eucharist by exploring the full chapter "Understanding the Eucharist Through the Seder." This lesson will guide individuals to internalize and discuss their insights in a group setting.

Lesson Plan

1. Opening Prayer (5 minutes)

Leader: Heavenly Father, we come before You with grateful hearts, having journeyed through the Seder meal and reflected on its deep significance. As we now turn to understanding the connection between the Seder and the Eucharist, open our hearts and minds to the truths You wish to reveal. May our discussions draw us closer to You and strengthen our faith. We ask this in the name of Jesus Christ, our Lord. Amen.

2. Introduction to the Lesson (5 minutes)

Leader: Today, we will reflect on the entire chapter "Understanding the Eucharist Through the Seder." We'll divide into four groups, with each group assigned to different sections of the chapter. After discussing their assigned sections, each group will share their insights with the larger group.

3. Group Reading (35 minutes)

Leader: Divide the participants into four groups and assign each group one of the following sections. Each group will spend 25 minutes discussing their section, followed by a 2-3 minute presentation to the larger group.

Group 1:

The Role of the Covenant, Anamnesis, and The Lighting of the Candles

- Discuss the significance of the covenant in both the Seder and the Eucharist.
- Explore the concept of sacred memory (anamnesis) and its power in both traditions.
- Reflect on the symbolism of the lighting of the candles as it relates to Christ, the Light of the World.

Group 2:

The First Cup, The Breaking of the Matzah, The Unleavened Bread, and The Second Cup

- Examine the meaning of the First Cup (Cup of Sanctification) in relation to our call to holiness.
- Discuss the symbolism of the breaking of the matzah (Afikoman) and its connection to Christ's sacrifice.
- Consider the significance of unleavened bread as a symbol of purity and sacrifice.
- Reflect on the Second Cup (Cup of Deliverance) and its fulfillment in the new covenant.

Group 3:

The Eating of Bitter Herbs, The Third Cup, and The Cup of Elijah

- Discuss the symbolism of the bitter herbs and their connection to Christ's suffering.
- Reflect on the Third Cup (Cup of Redemption) and its significance in the Eucharist.
- Explore the meaning of the Cup of Elijah in both the Seder and Christian anticipation of Christ's return.

Group 4:

The Fourth Cup, The Singing of the Hallel Psalms, The Passover Lamb, The Role of Family and Community, and The Concept of Sacrifice

- Examine the significance of the Fourth Cup (Cup of Praise) as it relates to the Eucharist and the heavenly banquet.
- Discuss the importance of the Hallel Psalms in praising God for deliverance.
- Reflect on the Passover lamb as a prefigurement of Christ, the Lamb of God.
- Explore the communal aspects of both the Seder and the Eucharist, focusing on the role of family and community.
- Discuss the concept of sacrifice in both the Seder and the Eucharist, particularly how Christ's sacrifice fulfills and transcends the Passover lamb.

Discussion Guidance

Each group will spend 25 minutes discussing their assigned sections, focusing on how the Seder has illuminated their understanding of the Eucharist. Afterward, each group will choose a spokesperson to share their insights.

4. Group Discussion (20 minutes)

Leader: Reconvene the groups and invite the spokesperson from each group to present their reflections. After each presentation, open the floor for additional comments and reflections.

Discussion Questions:

- How has the Seder meal deepened your understanding of the Eucharist?
- What new connections have you discovered between the two traditions?
- How will this experience influence your future participation in the Eucharist?
- In what ways has your appreciation for the covenant and Christ's sacrifice been enriched?

Encourage a meaningful discussion, allowing everyone to share their thoughts and insights.

5. Closing Prayer (5 minutes)

Leader: Gracious God, thank You for the rich insights and reflections we've shared today. As we go forth, may the connections we've discovered between the Seder and the Eucharist deepen our love and reverence for the Eucharist. Guide us to live out these truths in our daily lives, always mindful of the great sacrifice Christ made for us. We ask this in Jesus' name. Amen.

Conclusion

As we draw our journey to a close, we find ourselves enriched by a deeper understanding of the Eucharist through the lens of the Seder meal. This ancient Jewish tradition, filled with symbolism and meaning, has served as a powerful key, unlocking the profound mysteries of our Christian faith. By walking through the Seder, we have not only connected with the faith of our ancestors but have also seen how these traditions find their ultimate fulfillment in Christ.

The Seder meal is more than just a remembrance of the past; it is a living tradition that speaks to us today, bridging the old and the new. Each element of the meal—the lighting of the candles, the cups of wine, the breaking of the matzah, and the bitter herbs—points to the life, death, and resurrection of Jesus Christ. These symbols, rich in history, have been given new life through Christ, offering us a way to enter more fully into the mystery of the Eucharist.

Through this exploration, we have come to see the Eucharist not merely as a ritual but as a profound encounter with the living Christ. The bread and wine we partake in are not just reminders of Christ's sacrifice; they are a participation in His life, death, and resurrection. Each time we approach the altar, we are invited to step into the divine story—a story of love, redemption, and eternal life.

As you continue on your spiritual journey, may the insights gained from this study of the Seder meal deepen your love for the Eucharist. May you approach the altar with renewed reverence, awe, and gratitude, knowing that in the Eucharist, you are not just remembering Christ—you are encountering Him, receiving His grace, and being drawn into the fullness of His life.

The Eucharist is the source and summit of our Christian faith, a gift that continually nourishes and sustains us. It is the fulfillment of God's promises and a foretaste of the heavenly banquet to come. As you go forth, carry with you the richness of this tradition, and let it transform your understanding of the Eucharist, your relationship with Christ, and your life as a disciple.

May this journey through the Seder and the Eucharist inspire you to live more fully in the light of Christ's love, to share that love with others, and to remain ever close to the One who gave His life that we might live. Amen.

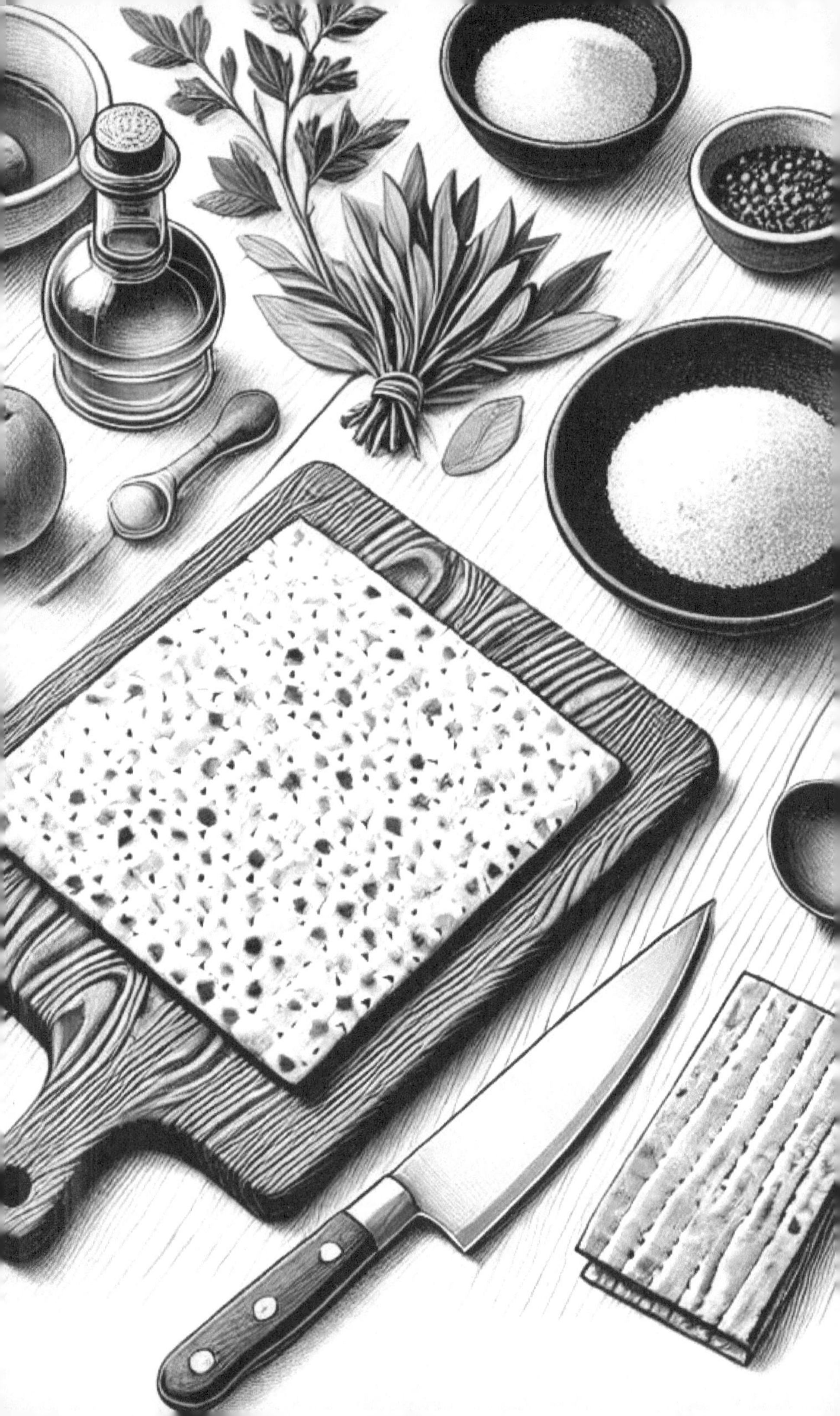

APPENDIX

Recipes

As we gather to celebrate the Passover meal, it is essential to prepare the traditional foods that carry deep symbolic meaning within the Jewish rite. This meal, rich in history and significance, connects us to the ancient traditions of our ancestors while also offering a profound reflection on our faith journey. The recipes provided here are carefully adjusted to serve 10 people, ensuring that everyone can partake in this sacred meal together.

Each recipe is crafted with attention to detail, ensuring that the meal is both abundant and symbolic. These dishes not only fulfill the requirements of the Seder but also allow us to engage deeply with the rich history of our faith. As you prepare and share this meal, may it bring you closer to understanding the profound connection between the Passover and the Eucharist, celebrating the fulfillment of God's promises through Christ.

Matzot (Unleavened Bread)

Ingredients for 10 pieces of matzot:

- 500g all-purpose flour
- Water (enough to form dough)
- A pinch of salt

Instructions:

1. Dissolve the salt in the water. Slowly add the water to the flour, kneading until you form a firm dough. Hand-kneading is preferred for better consistency.
2. Once the dough is ready, cover it and let it rest briefly. Roll out the dough with a rolling pin or stretch it by hand until it's about half a centimeter thick.
3. Cut the dough into small round pieces, enough for one or two per participant, with three larger pieces set aside for the Father.
4. Mark one of the larger pieces with a knife into segments according to the number of participants, making it easier to divide later.
5. Before baking, prick the matzot with a fork or knife and lightly dust them with flour.
6. Bake in a low oven until the dough forms a crust but does not harden.

Note: Prepare a few extra and three larger pieces of for the Father to use during the rite. Calculate that each person in the room will need to take a small piece from these larger ones.

Beżot (Eggs)

Ingredients:

- 10 eggs (one per participant)

Instructions:

1. Hard boil the eggs by placing them in a pot of water and bringing it to a boil. Once boiled, cool them in cold water and peel.
2. After peeling, lightly roast the eggs in a low oven until they develop a slight color.

Note: Prepare additional eggs in case some break and for those who might want extra.

Charoset

Ingredients for 10 people:

- 120g dried prunes
- 120g dates
- 60g almonds (peeled and dry)
- 3 apples (peeled and chopped)
- 2 cm piece of fresh ginger (peeled and chopped)
- 1/4 cup sweet red wine
- 1 tablespoon honey
- 1 tablespoon lemon juice
- Cinnamon to taste
- 2 tablespoons ground matzah

Instructions:

1. Finely chop the prunes, dates, almonds, apples, and ginger until they are in small pieces, but not a paste.

2. Mix in the wine, honey, lemon juice, and cinnamon, stirring until the mixture has a texture similar to clay.

3. If the mixture is too runny, add the ground matzah to thicken it.

4. This mixture can be prepared up to six hours in advance and stored covered in the refrigerator.

Roast Lamb

Ingredients:

- A whole lamb (size depending on the number of guests; approximately 1 kg of meat per 2 people)
- Traditional spices (garlic, pepper, fennel seeds, rosemary, etc.)
- Coarse salt
- Olive oil
- Water
- Onions (sliced)
- Aluminum foil (for covering)

Instructions:

1. **Preparation:** Start by thoroughly cleaning and gutting the lamb. Ensure that no bones are broken, in keeping with traditional practices. This step is important for maintaining the symbolic integrity of the sacrifice.

2. **Marination:** In a bowl, combine coarse salt, olive oil, and your chosen spices—such as garlic, pepper, fennel seeds, rosemary, and thyme. Mix until you have a well-blended marinade. Generously rub this mixture all over the lamb, making sure to coat it thoroughly. Allow the lamb to marinate for about an hour to absorb the flavors.

3. **Setting the Base:** In a large baking tray, create a bed of sliced onions. These will serve as a natural rack for the lamb and will also help to keep the meat moist throughout the long roasting process.

4. **Adding Moisture:** Pour a sufficient amount of water into the tray, just enough to cover the base. This water will steam during cooking, keeping the lamb tender and infusing it with the flavor of the onions.

5. **Covering:** Loosely cover the lamb with aluminum foil. This will help retain moisture and prevent the lamb from drying out during the lengthy roasting process.

6. **Roasting:** Roast the lamb in a wood-fired bread oven, if available, for approximately 8 hours. The cooking time may vary depending on the size of the lamb. If using a home oven, set it to a low temperature and monitor the lamb as it cooks, adjusting the time as needed. The goal is to achieve a tender, succulent roast that is cooked through without becoming dry.

7. **Serving Suggestions:** Once the lamb is perfectly roasted, serve it with roasted potatoes and a refreshing mint sauce. To prepare the mint sauce, simmer fresh mint leaves with water and sugar until the mixture is reduced to a syrupy consistency. This adds a traditional and flavorful complement to the lamb.

Notes:

- **Presentation:** The lamb should be served whole, with the head intact, as a powerful symbol of the unity of the family and the continuity of tradition. After roasting, keep the lamb warm and only bring it out right before eating. It is essential to maintain the ceremonial nature of the meal, and this includes the timing of when the lamb is presented.

- **The Lamb Shank Bone:** During the retelling of the Exodus story, the lamb shank bone (only the bone, not the meat) is used symbolically. This bone should be taken from the oven and placed at the center of the table at this point in the Seder. There will be approximately 15 minutes between this moment and the actual eating of the lamb. This time allows for the completion of the storytelling and enhances the anticipation of the meal.

- **Timing the Presentation:** The lamb can be brought out either at the point of the Exodus story or later during the time of eating, depending on the circumstances. Bringing the lamb out at the Exodus point allows the meat time to settle, which enhances its flavor and texture. However, if the environment is too cold and there is a risk that the lamb will become too cold in the 15 minutes before eating, it is perfectly acceptable to bring the lamb out during the actual meal. This ensures that the lamb is served warm and at its best.

- **Family Context Adaptation:** If this Seder is celebrated within a family context and preparing a whole lamb is not practical, you can use pieces of lamb instead. If the gathering is large, consider adding more lamb shanks to ensure there is enough meat for everyone. This adaptation maintains the symbolic significance of the lamb while making the meal more manageable for smaller or larger groups.

Glossary of Terms

Afikoman: A piece of matzah that is broken off during the Seder, hidden, and later eaten as the final food of the meal. It symbolizes the Paschal lamb that was eaten at the end of the meal during the time of the Temple.

Beẓot: The plural of *Beẓah*, which is the Hebrew word for egg. The egg used in the Seder symbolizes both the festival sacrifice brought in the Temple and the mourning for the destruction of the Temple.

Charoset: A sweet, brown mixture representing the mortar used by the Israelites in Egypt. Made from ingredients such as apples, nuts, wine, and cinnamon, it symbolizes the sweetness of freedom.

Haggadah: The text recited during the Seder, recounting the story of the Exodus from Egypt. It includes prayers, songs, and rituals that guide the participants through the Seder.

Hallel: A series of Psalms (113-118) sung during the Seder to praise God for His deliverance of Israel. It is divided into two parts during the Seder, one before and one after the meal.

Karpas: A vegetable, usually parsley, that is dipped in saltwater and eaten at the beginning of the Seder. It symbolizes the tears shed by the Israelites during their slavery in Egypt.

Matzah: Unleavened bread eaten during the Seder to commemorate the haste with which the Israelites left

Egypt, not having time to let their bread rise. It also symbolizes humility and freedom.

Maggid: The storytelling portion of the Seder where the Exodus story is recounted. It includes the Four Questions traditionally asked by the youngest participant.

Maror: Bitter herbs, typically horseradish, eaten during the Seder to symbolize the bitterness of slavery in Egypt.

Nirtzah: The concluding section of the Seder, during which a prayer is recited asking God to accept the Seder service, and the hope for next year in Jerusalem is expressed.

Pesach (Passover): The Jewish festival commemorating the Exodus from Egypt and the liberation of the Israelites from slavery. The Seder meal is the central ritual of Pesach.

Seder: The ritual meal conducted on the first night(s) of Passover, where the story of the Exodus is recounted, and symbolic foods are eaten. The word *Seder* means "order," reflecting the ordered sequence of the meal.

Z'roa: A roasted lamb shank bone placed on the Seder plate, symbolizing the Paschal lamb sacrificed in the Temple. It also represents God's "outstretched arm" in delivering the Israelites from Egypt.

Dayenu: A traditional Passover song meaning "It would have been enough," expressing gratitude for all the gifts God gave to the Jewish people, each of which would have been enough on its own.

Kiddush: A blessing recited over wine to sanctify the holiday or Sabbath, marking the beginning of sacred time.

Shehecheyanu: A blessing recited to thank God for enabling us to reach a special or new occasion. It is traditionally recited at the beginning of holidays and special events.

Eucharist: In Christian theology, the sacrament commemorating the Last Supper, in which bread and wine are consecrated and consumed. It represents Christ's sacrifice and His establishment of the New Covenant.

Church Documents on the Jewish Roots of the Eucharist

"Catechism of the Catholic Church" (1992): The "Catechism of the Catholic Church" provides an extensive overview of Catholic beliefs, including the Eucharist and its deep connection to the Jewish Passover. In particular, sections 1333-1336 explain how the Last Supper, celebrated during Passover, prefigures the Eucharist. These passages highlight the significance of the unleavened bread and the cup of blessing used in the Seder meal, showing how they are fulfilled in the sacrament of the Eucharist.

"Ecclesia de Eucharistia" (2003) by Pope John Paul II: This encyclical reflects on the centrality of the Eucharist in the life of the Church. In paragraphs 4-5 and 47, Pope John Paul II discusses the Last Supper in the context of the Jewish Passover, drawing a clear connection between the traditional Haggadah prayers and the words of Christ during the institution of the Eucharist. The document emphasizes how the Eucharist is both a memorial of Christ's sacrifice and a continuation of the Passover celebration.

"Lumen Gentium" (1964): In "Lumen Gentium," the Second Vatican Council explores the nature of the Church, particularly in relation to the Eucharist. Paragraphs 9 and

16 discuss how the Eucharist, rooted in the Jewish Passover, forms the heart of Christian worship. The document explains how the Eucharist is a fulfillment of the Old Testament Passover, making the Church a living continuation of Israel's covenant with God.

"Nostra Aetate" (1965): This declaration from Vatican II addresses the Church's relationship with non-Christian religions, with a particular emphasis on Judaism. It acknowledges the shared heritage between Jews and Christians and underscores the importance of understanding the Jewish roots of the Eucharist. "Nostra Aetate" encourages a deeper appreciation of the Seder meal as it relates to the Last Supper and the establishment of the New Covenant.

"Verbum Domini" (2010) by Pope Benedict XVI: This apostolic exhortation delves into the role of Scripture in the life of the Church. Paragraphs 40 and 54 highlight the connections between the Old and New Testaments, particularly how Jewish traditions, including the Passover, illuminate the meaning of the Eucharist. Pope Benedict XVI discusses how the readings and rituals of the Jewish Seder meal are echoed in the liturgical practices of the Eucharist, drawing believers into a deeper understanding of this sacred tradition.

Annotated Bibliography

1. **"Jesus and the Jewish Roots of the Eucharist: Unlocking the Secrets of the Last Supper" by Brant Pitre.** In this insightful book, Pitre explores the connections between the Jewish Passover meal and the Christian Eucharist. He delves into ancient Jewish traditions and Scripture to reveal how the Last Supper was rooted in the Jewish Seder and what it means for Christians today.

2. **"Our Father Abraham: Jewish Roots of the Christian Faith" by Marvin R. Wilson.** Wilson provides an in-depth look at the Jewish foundations of Christianity, emphasizing the cultural and religious context in which Jesus lived. This book is essential for understanding how Jewish traditions and beliefs have shaped Christian theology and practices.

3. **"Christ in the Passover: Why is This Night Different?" by Ceil and Moishe Rosen.** This book offers a detailed explanation of the Passover Seder and its significance for Christians. The authors, both Messianic Jews, show how the elements of the Seder point to Jesus Christ and His fulfillment of Old Testament prophecies.

4. **"The Jewish Roots of Christological Monotheism: Papers from the St. Andrews Conference on the Historical Origins of the Worship of Jesus" edited by Carey C. Newman, James R. Davila, and Gladys S. Lewis.** This scholarly collection explores the origins of Christ worship in early Christianity, examining how Jewish monotheism and beliefs influenced the development of

Christology. It's a valuable resource for those interested in the theological roots of Christian worship practices.

5. **"Feasts of the Bible: A Christian Guide to the Jewish Festivals" by Sam Nadler.** Nadler's book is a practical guide for Christians who want to understand the significance of Jewish festivals, including Passover. He explains how these feasts relate to the life and ministry of Jesus and how they can be observed by Christians today.

6. **"The Crucified Rabbi: Judaism and the Origins of Catholic Christianity" by Taylor R. Marshall.** Marshall examines the Jewish origins of many Catholic traditions, focusing on how Jesus, as a Jewish rabbi, fulfilled Jewish expectations of the Messiah. The book highlights the connections between Judaism and Catholicism, making it a useful resource for understanding the Seder's significance in Christian worship.

7. **"The Last Supper: What Really Happened" by Brant Pitre.** This book provides a detailed account of the Last Supper, focusing on its Jewish context and its significance for early Christians. Pitre argues that understanding the Last Supper as a Passover meal is key to understanding the Eucharist and its role in Christian worship.

8. **"Celebrating Biblical Feasts: In Your Home or Church" by Martha Zimmerman.** Zimmerman's book is a practical guide for Christians interested in observing the biblical feasts, including Passover, in their homes or churches. She offers step-by-step instructions for celebrating these feasts in a way that honors their Jewish roots while embracing Christian faith.

9. "The New Passover: The Life of Christ in the Light of the Jewish Passover" by Heinrich Schlier. Schlier's work explores how the Jewish Passover provides a framework for understanding the life, death, and resurrection of Jesus Christ. This book offers a theological perspective on how the Seder and the Eucharist are connected in Christian thought.

10. "The Seder: Its Evolution and History" by Hayyim Schauss. Schauss provides a comprehensive history of the Seder, tracing its development from ancient times to the present day. This book is essential for understanding how the Seder has evolved and how its various elements have been interpreted over the centuries.

Clarifications on the Practice of the Christian Seder Meal

In this appendix, we will address some of the concerns and controversies surrounding the Christian adaptation of the Seder meal, a practice that has been met with both interest and caution within various Christian communities. By understanding these issues, we can ensure that our engagement with the Seder is both respectful of Jewish tradition and faithful to Christian theology.

Historical Controversies

- **Cultural Appropriation Concerns**: Some Jewish communities have raised concerns about Christians adopting the Seder meal, seeing it as a form of cultural appropriation. It's essential to approach the Seder with sensitivity, acknowledging its origins and significance in Judaism. Christians should recognize the Seder as a Jewish tradition and be careful not to misrepresent or trivialize it.
- **Theological Concerns**: Certain theologians have expressed caution, arguing that the Seder is a Jewish ritual that points to the coming of the Messiah, which Christians believe has already been fulfilled in Jesus Christ. There is concern that Christians participating in the Seder might blur the lines between the Old Covenant and the New Covenant. To address this, it's

important to clarify that the Christian Seder is not a replacement for the Eucharist but a way to deepen understanding of its roots.
- **Liturgical Concerns**: Within the Church, there has been debate over whether the Seder should be incorporated into Christian liturgy. The official stance is that while it can be celebrated in educational or communal settings, it should not replace or be confused with the liturgical celebration of the Eucharist. The Seder can serve as a tool for catechesis but must remain distinct from the sacraments.

Defending the Practice

- **Educational Value**: The Christian Seder, when conducted with the right intent, can serve as a powerful educational tool, helping believers understand the Jewish roots of the Christian faith and the deeper meaning of the Eucharist. By participating in the Seder, Christians can gain insight into how Jesus, as a Jew, lived and celebrated, thereby enriching their appreciation of the New Testament.
- **Respectful Adaptation**: To ensure that the Seder is practiced respectfully, it's crucial to adapt it in a way that acknowledges its Jewish roots while highlighting its fulfillment in Christ. This means clearly differentiating between the traditional Jewish Seder and the Christian reflection on it, focusing on the typology that sees Christ as the fulfillment of the Passover lamb.
- **Support from Church Documents**: The Church encourages the study of Jewish traditions to better understand Christianity's own heritage. Documents

such as "Nostra Aetate" highlight the shared spiritual heritage of Christians and Jews and promote mutual respect and understanding. Engaging with the Seder in a thoughtful and respectful manner aligns with these teachings.

- **Pastoral Sensitivity**: For pastors and lay leaders, it's essential to approach the Seder with pastoral sensitivity. This includes educating participants about its origins, its place within Jewish life, and how it points to the Eucharist. When done properly, the Seder can deepen the faith of participants without causing confusion or offense.

Conclusion

Including a Christian reflection on the Seder in this book is meant to enhance understanding and appreciation of the Eucharist, not to diminish or appropriate Jewish traditions. By following the guidelines outlined in this appendix, you can confidently engage with the Seder, knowing that you are participating in a practice that is both theologically sound and respectful of its origins.

About the Author

Fr. Dominic Michael Sultana (b. 1980) hails from Malta, Europe. Responding to his call to the priesthood, he entered the local Diocesan Seminary and was ordained in 2005.

For the past two decades, he has dedicated his life to researching and implementing effective ways to spread the Gospel. His journey has taken him to various countries, including Malta, Italy, the USA, Canada, Australia, New Zealand, Ireland, Nigeria, the Czech Republic, and the United Kingdom, for study, ministry, and experience.

He served as the Vice Rector of Ta' Pinu National Shrine for 8 years and as a parish priest. He is the founder of God Mediation Ministry and a member of the Global 2033 Committee. He holds a Doctorate in Sacred Theology (Rome), a 3-year diploma in Spiritual Counseling, and is an Advanced Practitioner in Cognitive Coaching.

For more books by Fr. Dominic, scan the QR code on the right.

To visit his website https://www.godmediation.world/, scan the QR code on the left.

Made in United States
Troutdale, OR
03/15/2025